"If you're looking to grow your business, *Million-Dollar Passion* is a must-read. The tools in this book can help you build a brand and rapidly grow your business year after year, all while achieving work-life balance and having fun."

—**Tonia DeCosimo**, CEO, *P.O.W.E.R. Magazine* and P.O.W.E.R. Network

"Victoria Wieck is a woman to be lauded, admired, and emulated! She is a '3-P' powerhouse of passion, positive energy, and persistence! Other things I can throw in, for good measure, are 'wisdom,' 'resolve,' 'fortitude,' 'courage,' and just plain 'guts'! All of these have created the private and public success that Victoria is today. Victoria's book, *Million-Dollar Passion*, is a must-read, not only for those who wish to explore new ventures of any kind but for those who long to discover and utilize some of the intrinsic qualities born of true creativity combined with true leadership. Victoria teaches the magic of her trade in easy-to-understand terms that can be adjusted and customized to anyone in any situation. Her self-learned formulas and her highs and lows are generously shared and explained. The result is eye-opening experiences and an excellent foundation that will motivate and help actualize a true sense of empowerment."

—**Princess Amanda Borghese**

"The American Dream is more achievable than ever. *Million-Dollar Passion* is a must-read. There is the American dream, and there is the lottery. Please don't confuse them. The American Dream is only there if you put in the hard work to make it happen. Victoria is a shining example of how much hard work and dedication can achieve—she is focused, strong, and determined. In this book, you will see how you need to have all these traits to succeed with your career and family. Amazing story and an amazing lady. Well done, Victoria!"

—**Daniel Green**, celebrity chef; TV host; and author of *Paleo Monday to Friday, Modern Dining for Life,* and eleven other cookbooks

"I can't say enough about Victoria's unwavering commitment and passion in helping entrepreneurs grow their businesses with her book, *Million-Dollar Passion.* I have been so fortunate to have had Victoria personally help me improve and grow my business by utilizing many of the tools and strategies mentioned in her book. It has been a game-changer for me and my business! So, don't miss out on this step-by-step guide on how to grow and maximize your business success. Thank you, Victoria, for your unique insights and invaluable advice! I am sure *Million-Dollar Passion* will help many more entrepreneurs to realize their potential."

—**Katherine Sempecos**, CEO, Prism Med Spa

"Everyone needs a friend and mentor to encourage and motivate them. In this book, Victoria honestly shares her journey, insights, and strategies in a raw way. Hard work and determination are key ingredients for success, but not the entire recipe. I recommend *Million-Dollar Passion* for those looking for the rest of the recipe. It provides practical, actionable steps that readily apply to help you move forward with clarity and intention—well done!"

—**Michele Lau**, gemstone and jewelry expert, QVC

"It is a true honor and privilege to endorse Victoria Wieck's inaugural book, as it holds a special significance. Victoria's unwavering guidance and support played a pivotal role in instilling the courage and expertise necessary for me to embark on my own passionate journey, resulting in the successful launch of my dream business just last year. Her extraordinary humility and generosity shine through in every aspect of her work. Her selfless dedication to empowering countless individuals like myself to pursue their dreams is awe-inspiring. Victoria has forged her path to prosperity and paved the way for millions of others to find their own entrepreneurial success and fulfillment with this priceless guidance. May her legacy continue to resonate and inspire generations through this book."

—**Caprice Crebar**, CEO, Heart Link Network Worldwide

"Incredible, inspirational, and a must-read! Victoria Wieck is an absolute queen that puts the 'power' in 'empowerment' as she delves into the very essence of human potential, exploring the multifaceted dimensions of the power, purpose, and resilience that lies within each and every one of us. In this inspiring tale of resilience, Wieck weaves an enthralling narrative, chronicling her journey to achieving enviable wealth and prosperity all while balancing success with family. Readers will believe that they too can achieve multifaceted success while balancing ambition with the pursuit of fulfilling a healthy family life. It's a testament to the fact that wealth and success need not come at the expense of family bonds but can, in fact, strengthen them. *Million-Dollar Passion* isn't just a blueprint for financial success; it's a road map for personal growth, self-discovery, and finding purpose. The authenticity of Wieck's voice inspires one to dream big and reach for the stars! *Million-Dollar Passion* is not only a compelling story of achievement but also an uplifting and motivational guide for anyone who dares to dream big!"

—**Tsikki Thau**, author; stress management expert; and founder of the S.N.A.P. Instant Stress Relief Technique

"Whether you're an entrepreneur seeking a profitable side hustle or a business owner searching for practical solutions to the growing needs of your business, Victoria's improbable but highly successful entrepreneurship journey offers valuable lessons. The tools and solutions in this book are simple and unique and can be applied to any modern business. Victoria's ability to creatively solve the numerous problems that modern business owners face shines through in this book."

—**Susan Bell Bien,** former international investment banker, Citicorp: Tokyo, San Francisco, and New York, and author of *The Art of Redemption* and *The Wisdom Keepers*

MILLION-DOLLAR PASSION

MILLION-DOLLAR PASSION

*How to Turn Your Idea into a
Multimillion-Dollar Business*

VICTORIA WIECK

JEFFREY A. MANGUS, EDITOR

ROWMAN & LITTLEFIELD
Lanham • Boulder • New York • London

Published by Rowman & Littlefield
An imprint of The Rowman & Littlefield Publishing Group, Inc.
4501 Forbes Boulevard, Suite 200, Lanham, Maryland 20706
www.rowman.com

86-90 Paul Street, London EC2A 4NE

British Library Cataloguing in Publication Information Available

Library of Congress Cataloging-in-Publication Data
Names: Wieck, Victoria, author.
Title: Million-dollar passion : how to turn your idea into a multimillion-dollar business /
   Victoria Wieck.
Description: Lanham : Rowman & Littlefield, [2024] | Includes bibliographical
   references and index.
Identifiers: LCCN 2023023581 (print) | LCCN 2023023582 (ebook) |
   ISBN 9781538180921 (cloth ; alk. paper) | ISBN 9781538180938 (ebook)
Subjects: LCSH: New business enterprises. | Entrepreneurship. | Success in business.
Classification: LCC HD62.5 .W4877 2024 (print) | LCC HD62.5 (ebook) |
   DDC 658.1/1—dc23/eng/20230706
LC record available at https://lccn.loc.gov/2023023581
LC ebook record available at https://lccn.loc.gov/2023023582

CONTENTS

CONTENTS

FOREWORD

Ken Hicks

Victoria Wieck was one of the most impressive TV personalities I met during my time as the executive vice president of the Home Shopping Network (HSN). While it was clear that she was a talented jewelry designer, her astonishing success required much more than talent and passion. Even though I moved on to pursue other endeavors—accepting the CEO position at Academy Sports + Outdoors—I've kept a great friendship with Victoria over the following years and have watched her and her company grow. I am amazed by her ability to generate incredible business opportunities with her creativity and innovativeness. But what makes Victoria really special is her character—her honesty, persistence, and willingness to work hard. I've watched her build and grow her jewelry brand from its infancy to an internationally recognized brand, even during some of the most challenging times: the global financial crisis in 2008 and the COVID-19 pandemic. She adapted, evolved, elevated, and innovated to keep growing her business to the next level.

Victoria's journey from a penniless immigrant to a highly successful businesswoman is a story that will inspire anyone who dares to dream. In a recent conversation I had with her, she explained why she wrote this book. She believes that anything is possible if you have passion, work hard, and believe in yourself. She understands that the road to entrepreneurship is paved with obstacles, but she also knows how to stay motivated, persistent, resilient, and creative to overcome all the challenges you may face. She wants to share her story so others can achieve their dreams. Without a doubt, this is the book Victoria wishes she had at the beginning of her journey.

Whether you are thinking about starting a business or you want to grow a small business you've already started, you will find Victoria's tips highly applicable and achievable. In this book, she shares how to unleash your passion, identify the best opportunity to monetize it, select your ideal target audience, and perfect the best methods to sell your product. While many entrepreneurship books offer theoretical advice full of modern-day buzzwords, this book is full of real-life stories and examples that you can really use in your business. True to character, Victoria shares details about some of the worst mistakes she's made in her career and the lessons she learned from them. Some of the most valuable tips range from testing marketing concepts before spending valuable dollars to compelling storytelling techniques you can apply to your business. As a small business owner, storytelling is one of the most effective ways to generate sales and differentiate yourself from the competition. Victoria is an expert storyteller whose techniques are unique, refreshing, and effective. How do I know? In the TV retail business, all brands and TV personalities are judged by their sales dollars per minute and their ability to connect with their audience. Victoria's storytelling skills are exceptional at captivating the customer's attention and capturing their loyalty. Throughout the book, you will find her "secret sauce" to mastering the multiple skills needed to grow and scale your business.

During my career as the CEO of Academy Sports + Outdoors, the CEO of Footlocker, and the president of JCPenney, among other positions, I've met many entrepreneurs. But I can't think of a better person than Victoria Wieck to write a book on turning your passion into a lucrative dream business. Victoria did exactly that, and *Million-Dollar Passion* gives everyone who wants to build a business the tools to do the same.

Ken Hicks

CEO of Academy Sports + Outdoors
Former CEO of Foot Locker
Former president of JCPenney
Former president of Payless ShoeSource
Former executive vice president of HSN
Former director of Whole Foods Market

Graduate of Harvard Business School
Graduate of the United States Military Academy at West Point

INTRODUCTION

The American Dream is the opportunity to pursue your true passion and make enough money to live your life to its full potential. It is also the opportunity to help others, including your children, to pursue their passions and achieve their dreams without social or cultural barriers.
—DR. HAN J. LEE, ACUPUNCTURE AND ORIENTIAL MEDICINE, AUTHOR'S FATHER

THE AMERICAN DREAM. YOU HEAR THE EXPRESSION ALMOST everywhere, but what exactly is the essence of living the American Dream? Is it quitting your job and building a multimillion dollar business, much like those built by Bill Gates, Steve Jobs, and Jeff Bezos? Or perhaps you are a single parent seeking to provide a bright future for your children, and that's your idea of the American Dream. For many, simply earning enough money to buy a house and a car, enough to earn a living and raise a family is the American Dream, but there is more at stake here than meets the eye.

During the Great Depression, James Truslow Adams coined the phrase "American Dream" in his 1931 book *Epic of America.* He wrote, "But there has also been the American Dream, that dream of a land in which life should be better and richer and fuller for every man, with opportunity for each according to his ability or achievement."[1] Once the Great Depression was over, many young people pursued the American Dream by making opportunities for success. However, according to Adams, success was defined by earning substantial amounts of money. Yet, for many people, the American Dream meant something entirely different. It was more than money for many, more about family and happiness, along with freedom to choose and pursue one's own dreams.

I discovered my personal American Dream as I focused on my family, my passion, and making enough money to save for a rainy day. My dream started when I was a hopeful little girl in a small coastal town in South Korea. I'll never forget standing with my parents, looking beyond the horizon, across the ocean, believing that in America, the land of opportunity, all my dreams would come true. Considered affluent in South Korea, my parents had a delightful house on the beach, provided private school education for their children, and paid a cook to prepare meals for the family. It was expected for well-off families to send their girls to college to earn female-friendly degrees, such as home economics, music, or art. In South Korea, every young girl's future was limited to being a wife and mother. Even though financially sound, my parents dreamed of moving their family to America, where all four of their daughters, and their son, could be free to reach their full potentials.

When they acted upon this dream, however, and moved our family to America, the authorities of South Korea froze my family's fortune, leaving us with only thirty dollars in my father's pocket. With seven mouths to feed, needing money for food and shelter, my parents immediately took many jobs, and every day, our American Dream seemed to slip farther and farther away.

We were all thrust into a new world—having to learn a new language, adapt to a new culture. My siblings and I navigated all this while attending school. As the oldest, I was expected to also care for my four younger siblings. And worse, being in a new country as a young Korean woman, I faced ugly bigotry, discrimination, hypocrisy, and soon felt hopeless and deeply depressed.

Even through the devastating lows, I fought hard to persevere, and after high school, I earned degrees in economics from the University of California, Los Angeles and an MBA in finance and marketing from the University of Southern California. However, even with my high-level education, I could barely find a good job in Los Angeles. I searched for numerous high-paying jobs and was offered many excellent opportunities in New York City, but I couldn't bring myself to move away from my family.

When I met my husband, I took a temporary position in the marketing department of a jewelry company. And while I soon grew to love the job and became quite adept at it, I found myself exhausted, stressed, and numb from driving more than three hours day in and day out and working twelve- to fourteen-hour days. My husband wanted children, but I never envisioned myself pregnant, let alone taking care of toddlers on top of my long daily commute and work hours. My life had become a closed book and I didn't see a way out until one afternoon, while stopped in bumper-to-bumper traffic, I had a life-altering epiphany. I realized that I was devoting my entire life to building someone else's American Dream, and it was time to stand firm, take charge, and alter the course of my life. I knew, in that moment, that I had to try something different, but what? My husband and I were not wealthy, and the thought of draining what little money we had to start our own business was not a realistic option. However, I searched my soul and asked myself, *Why I am I here and what is my real purpose in life?* It was in that spectacular moment that something switched in my heart, filling me with an ever-present belief that I wasn't born to starve, be miserable, and merely exist. And it was in those precious, soul-stirring moments I knew my life was about to change—forever.

My road to success was paved with challenges. As I created Victoria Wieck Jewelry, I often worried if I was going to make it or if I was going to sink and drown. However, no matter what I have been through, I believe more than ever that the American Dream is attainable and within everyone's grasp. Here in *Million-Dollar Passion: How to Turn Your Idea into a Multimillion-Dollar Business*, I intend to show that with a phone, computer, and a few dollars, you can start your own business and, most of all, rise above the fray—and genuinely succeed—no matter who you are. The world around us is more interconnected than ever, and access to a global marketplace exists right in the palm of your hand. You do not need a fancy education, loads of money, or an "inside" connection, and you don't even need to be an expert in a particular field. Instead, you need a great idea backed by desire, perseverance, and passion. With *Million-Dollar Passion*, I intend to help you discover your genuine gift and identify your true mission in life. I'll help you realize the essential methods to turn your ideas or hobby into a highly profitable business, side hustle, or perhaps a multimillion-dollar empire. Within these pages, you will learn to test your idea before taking financial risks and uncover the inner workings of starting and operating your business on a budget. In addition, you will learn the essential ways to market your business to your target audience and learn how to scale your business to attain sustainable growth.

Remember, a seventeen-year-old started Subway with only $1,000; two teachers with only $1,000 founded Starbucks; and Google, Facebook, Microsoft, and Apple were started with less than $5,000. These companies grew through hard work, passion, and a powerful belief in achieving the American Dream. So think about how you may be that person who starts the next big thing that changes life as we know it. Allow me to help you be *indispensable*.

Let's get started!

Chapter 1

Envisioning the Dream

Every great dream begins with a dreamer. Always remember,
you have within you the strength, the patience, and the pas-
sion to reach for the stars, to change the world.

—Unknown

Dreams, aspirations, and passion are the cornerstones of
every business. However, for any business, large or small, to thrive,
grow, and prosper, one specific element must be in place from the
beginning: a clear vision. A distinct and achievable vision adds
form and substance to the desired end game—*success*. Unless an
entrepreneur has a powerful vision, their business will lose focus
and direction, eventually veering off course. Unfortunately, most
entrepreneurs fail because they spend inordinate amounts of time
chasing brass rings that do not follow their visions. Even though
opportunities may seem appealing, if they don't merge with your
vision or dreams, you must resist spending time on them; if they
do not contribute to your vision, it could be a waste of time.

When I started my company, Ravello Beverly Hills, I
envisioned providing high-quality fine jewelry for the modern
woman. However, I was often tempted to offer other products
that did not contribute to my vision. To my great regret, brass

rings I chased over the years included Ravello Beverly Hills perfume and Ravello Beverly Hills handbags. These products barely paid for themselves and did not contribute to my original vision. In fact, I couldn't have chosen more contradictory products if I had tried. Fine jewelry thrives on being timeless, something that transcends generations, while handbags and perfumes change seasonally. I wasted a lot of time, money, and effort on these products.

Chairman and CEO of General Electric, Jack Welch, once said, "Good business leaders create a vision, articulate the vision, passionately own the vision, and relentlessly drive it to completion."[1] A solid vision statement must be created as a foundational guide for your endeavor. It begins with implementing plans based on a distinct objective or idea and involves positioning your new business as something that will last for many years. There is no need to look farther than your cell phone, computer, or the world around you for examples of companies adhering to their vision statements and achieving outstanding results. For example, one of Google's missions is "to provide access to the world's information in one click."[2] Or consider the vision statement from Instagram: "Capture and share the world's moments."[3] In addition, LinkedIn has a distinct statement that appeals to anyone seeking career opportunities: "Create an economic opportunity for every member of the global workforce."[4]

These companies demonstrate how imperative a vision statement can be to building longevity, internal unity, brand recognition, and substantial financial success. A vision statement should always be the driving force, no matter how large or small your business may be. It will serve as its North Star, keeping you on the right track and preventing you from making inappropriate decisions. Now, more than ever, customers expect businesses to *solve problems* (a need) or *fulfill a desire* (a want). Wherever possible, that should at least be part of the message. For example, here are the ways Google, Instagram, and LinkedIn solve problems or fulfill desires:

- Google (Mostly) Solves a Problem: *I'm having trouble finding certain information I need for my project.*
- Instagram (Mostly) Fulfills a Desire: *I would like a social media site that only posts photographs.*
- LinkedIn (Mostly) Solves a Problem: *I must find a job because I need to pay my rent.*

To write a strong vision statement, conduct a brainstorming session—with just yourself—in a private, comfortable space. Ask yourself, *What do I truly believe?* Then examine yourself from within and observe the traits that make you unique. For example, do you believe in freedom, liberty, honesty, trustworthiness, steadfastness, or something else?

Next, ask yourself, *What small or large impact will my company have on the world?* Fuel your brainstorming session by using the identified beliefs and traits to describe what your company should stand for. You can write your answers on a whiteboard, in a journal, on a notepad, sticky notes, or index cards, or record or videotape your thoughts. No matter what your chosen method, it must be one that works for you. No two people are alike when it comes to the creative process. Note: Ensure your ideas are saved and backed up somewhere, so they may be referred to and refined later. If you happen to choose a whiteboard, don't forget to use your cell phone's camera to take a picture of your work.

Allow some time to pass—a couple of days or even a week—so your ideas can settle. Then, go back to your work with a clear mind and eliminate any words that do not reflect your company's vision and values. Then, build your vision statement around the remaining words or thoughts. Remember that it does not need to be a four-page master's thesis; use simple, direct words anyone can understand that empower your company forward. Sometimes it requires extra diligence to wordsmith the vision into those few precious words that capture and communicate everything in your dream. Succinctness is crucial, as is delivering a positive message to benefit others.

Passion-SMAART

Today, many human resource departments utilize the standard SMART goal approach—*Specific, Measurable, Achievable, Relevant,* and *Time-Bound*—when it comes to annual employee goal setting. However, through my entrepreneurial trials, I have discovered an added element—a secret weapon, if you will—that has made a significant difference throughout my career: *SMAART* goal setting. This acronym stands for *Specific, Measurable, Attainable, **Aspirational**, Relevant,* and *Time-Bound*. The extra "A" for *Aspirational* can make all the difference in succeeding at an entrepreneurial goal (versus an employee performance goal at a corporation).

- **S**pecific: What do you want to accomplish?
- **M**easurable: What metric(s) will you use to determine whether the effort is successful?
- **A**ttainable: Is the goal a stretch for you but realistic to achieve?
- **A**spirational: How will this goal tap into your passion and motivate you? If it doesn't, you won't have enough interest to achieve the goal.
- **R**elevant: How does the goal relate to accomplishing your vision?
- **T**ime-Bound: When is the deadline for the goal? What are the target benchmark dates along the way toward completing the goal?

An example of a SMAART goal would be to *build a dynamic commercial website* [specific] *by November 1 of this year* [time-bound] *that showcases the exciting* [aspirational] *launch of our new shoe line* [relevant] *and receives ten thousand visitors* [measurable] *in the first month* [time-bound].

Each letter from the acronym has been addressed in the above goal with one notable exception: *attainable*. Therefore, these goal-setting criteria can only be evaluated after the written statement. Be sure to include all the dimensions of the goal—the actions, deadlines, time commitments, and potential financial commitments. At that time, you can evaluate your goal in its totality.

It is crucial to recognize that a goal won't be achieved if it isn't well thought out, carefully planned, adequately funded and resourced, and properly implemented. Unlike your vision and passion, a goal must be relentlessly pursued and monitored. Mistakes and delays will likely occur if your attention isn't laser-focused.

Execution of a SMAART goal requires more than putting together a to-do list. It must be memorialized and tracked in multiple ways: a whiteboard, planning and strategy documents and spreadsheets, and calendar reminders (including the benchmark dates). Some individuals are more diligent than others in this regard but don't leave anything to chance. If it's important enough to itemize as a goal, it should be prioritized because it appears everywhere you might look regularly. I have witnessed too many companies fail because they do not follow a goal execution plan, monitor it, and initiate some method of whip-cracking to ensure compliance.

In 1968, American psychologist Edwin Locke published a scientific paper titled "Toward a Theory of Task Motivation and Incentives," which included his groundbreaking goal-setting theory.[5] This theory proved the direct correlation between goal setting and productivity. Furthermore, it demonstrated that setting goals with strategic productivity methods provided motivation leading to successful task completion and sparked extra engagement among team members.

In my case, I have found that once I've established a SMAART goal and rigidly monitored its progress, I have been able to stay the course and execute the goal. Don't get me wrong: It's not always easy! It's hard work creating a sustainable business with a strong foundation. Business owners who "wing it" might make some money out of the starting gate from a strong product or service, marketing/sales savvy, plain luck, or a combination of all three, but the business won't survive in the long run if its nuts and bolts aren't tightly fastened in place.

If you have a strong vision and are passionate about your business, you should have more than enough mojo to accomplish any SMAART goal and combat any problem or setback that arises—whether from an outside source or of your own making. If it's the latter, don't beat yourself up! *Everyone* makes mistakes. How you handle them, learn from them, and press onward distinguishes successes from failures.

As we'll cover later in this book, starting your own business venture can be terrifying. It's normal to be scared. In the beginning, there are many unknowns. You may feel like you are always on shaky ground and things could collapse at any moment. Take a deep breath. Relax. While you always want to maintain a high passion for your vision, you want to remove emotion from the day-to-day routines, which can negatively influence your decision-making.

I guarantee that if you stay true to your inherent core values and allow your passion and positive energy to shine through, the rest will come together. You have a choice: either do the foundational hard work and ride what might be a bumpy takeoff, or do nothing and have regrets for the rest of your life. It is 100 percent up to you. If you desire to reach the pinnacle of success—build a multimillion-dollar business from the ground up—you must do everything you can to execute daily, monthly, weekly, and long-term goals. If you stumble, get back up, learn from your mistakes, and continue. When you've made your first million, who will care about the disasters that occurred in the early stages? No one, especially not you.

I believe that a life without a dream can feel unrewarding and empty. We only have 86,400 seconds in a day, no more and no less. What are you going to do to fill that precious time? Will you be productive and create something that can grow over time, build wealth, and perhaps even establish a legacy that will last for future generations?

Hockey legend Wayne Gretzky once said, "You miss 100 percent of the shots you don't take."[6] So take as many shots as you can, *while you can*. The world is waiting to see what wonderful things you will bring to life.

KEY TAKEAWAYS

- If you stay true to your inherent core values and allow your passion and positive energy to shine through, the rest will come together.

- If you have a strong vision and are passionate about your business, you should have more than enough mojo to accomplish any SMAART goal and combat any problem or setback that arises.

- It is crucial to recognize that a goal won't be achieved if it isn't well thought out, carefully planned, adequately funded and resourced, and properly implemented.

CHAPTER 2

Kicking Your Fear

*Being aware of your fear is smart. Overcoming it is the mark
of a successful person.*[1]

—SETH GODIN

I GREW UP IN A SMALL SEASIDE VILLAGE IN SOUTH KOREA IN AN
upper-middle-class family. My father, an acupuncturist, and my
mother, a stay-at-home mom, instilled in me early on that happiness can be achieved by holding onto five key factors in life—
health, high-quality relationships, integrity, wealth, and longevity
of life—not our fears.

When my family immigrated to the United States, I was
more than afraid. I was excited and petrified. My father only
had about thirty dollars to his name, and we were all frightened
because we didn't have a home. Despite being a strong woman, my
mother was more frightened than I have ever seen her, so much
so that she was ready to leave, return to Korea, and start over—all
out of fear.

Being the oldest of five siblings, I had more than my share of
frightening and intimidating things to face. I had to learn a new
language as well as adapt to peer pressure and new cultures and
traditions, all while caring for my younger siblings.

My father knew I faced a ton of pressure adapting to my new life, gaining friends, and learning English, so he'd wake up early every morning before work, no matter how hard his life was, and circle words in the dictionary for me to memorize and learn. I'll never forget that. His dedication to his family was incredible, despite working three jobs. It was my father's way of showing me that I didn't have to be afraid and could do anything I wanted if I set my mind to it. And somehow, through it all, I never gave up. I felt that no matter how difficult my life was, I had my family, love, health, and a new life ahead. And even though we were poor, our family remained strong together. So, I vowed never to let anything compromise my integrity and was determined to conquer my fears and achieve true happiness. Even though my English was poor and I had low self-esteem and few friends, I soon discovered that the only way I could live a fulfilling life was to face my fears, recognize the triggers, overcome them, and do my absolute best.

FEAR OF FAILURE

You've probably heard the adage, "The only constant in life is change." But if change is the only constant in life, why are new business owners and entrepreneurs so bad at coping with it? The answer lies in one word: *fear*.

The first step in understanding and kicking your fear is knowing what fears you will face when starting a new business. Many factors can affect you, such as the fear of not having enough expertise or the fear of failure. Thirty-one percent of Americans fear failure, and according to recent research, fear of failure ranks higher than the fear of spiders and the fear of public speaking.[2] Fear of failure can negatively affect people's lives by discouraging risk-taking and hindering their pursuit of their dreams. Changing your perspective and mindset about failure is critical in overcoming the fear of failure. Failure isn't terrible—it's an opportunity for growth and learning. You can learn from your mistakes if you embrace them, and in my experience, mistakes are necessary ingredients for your eventual success.

I used every mistake and failure as a learning experience, as real-world training that showed me the ropes in building my business. I am living proof that overcoming the fear of failure is possible by taking small steps and not trying to accomplish everything all at once. Instead, organize your goals into small, manageable steps, focus on one thing at a time, and celebrate each of your small successes as they arrive.

IMPOSTOR SYNDROME AND FEAR

It's intimidating to start a new business for assorted reasons: fear of the unknown, financial insecurity, irregular work hours, the opinions of those around you, or the feeling you aren't worthy or that you don't have the skills to make your business a success. These are symptoms of a pattern of intrusive thinking known as impostor syndrome, which can lead to negative self-talk, self-doubt, and missed opportunities.

The feeling of being an impostor can affect anyone at any time, but perfectionists, hard workers, and high achievers are more likely to experience it. It happens when you doubt your abilities, worth, and merit in a role, which then provokes fear, anxiety, and stress. To combat these feelings, consider this: While you likely know enough about your product or service to answer most questions and resolve most issues, you don't need to know everything. If you don't know something, you can learn it. Continued education is essential for growth. So wear the "expert" label, strive to be your best, and overcome the fear of impostor syndrome.

FEAR OF NAYSAYERS

Along your journey there will be many naysayers and those who consider your actions crazy. Starting a business will seem crazy to many people, and they will be right—at first. Going out on a limb, believing in your abilities, and convincing others to buy into them, *is* crazy—and good for you. Embrace your craziness and appreciate it for what it is. Those willing to take risks make a difference in the world.

Show up and deliver outstanding products or services no matter how doubtful you are that people will respond well to your business. Remove their doubt through actionable products, services, and results. When you have a strong work ethic and service, no one can argue with it. People will eventually learn to believe in your results, even if they don't believe in you at first.

FEAR OF FAILING THE FAMILY

It might be frightening to think your new venture won't provide for your family or that it will become an embarrassment You might fear having less time with your family than you imagined. However, putting your family first and giving your all to your new venture will change your perspective and allow people to see your passion. Reassure your family members that you will never compromise their way of life as you embark on this venture (and make sure you don't). Talk to them openly about the risks and the importance of investing time and energy in the business's success. Ensure your family is prepared for the time and energy you will most likely spend on your business by clearly communicating the potential rewards—financial and emotional—the potential workload, as well as the risks involved. They know you better than anyone else. Ask them for help whenever appropriate and to walk this journey with you. One strategy that might help is to set clear boundaries for your business and for your family. For example, I set aside the hours between 2:30 and 5:00 p.m. each afternoon to spend with my children when they were young. This was possible partly due to the fact that many of my customers were located on the East Coast, which was three hours ahead of my hometown of Los Angeles. This also meant that I started my day a couple of hours earlier and worked right through lunch. I admit I probably lost some business, but I don't regret my decision.

KICKING YOUR FEAR

Among the most underrated, overlooked, yet essential skills for budding entrepreneurs is the ability to overcome fear. It is a learned skill, and one that is critical to understanding and implementing a strategy to address any fears or apprehension in starting or managing your business. Getting started or growing a business isn't about having money or time but taking the daunting first steps.

When starting a business, it is common to be paralyzed by fear, but it is extremely difficult to recognize this when it's actually happening. Our fear and inaction are often blamed on a lack of skills, money, time, and/or networks, or, sometimes, it's just plain procrastination. However, if we dig deeper, we'll find that fear is what is actually stopping us. If you let it, fear can stop you from starting your business, as it can prevent you from taking the necessary steps, having the difficult conversations, and making the big decisions.

Many fears we experience are subconscious, which makes identifying them difficult. Fear has been ingrained in our DNA as a safeguard from real dangers, and not listening to it can feel like going against our natural tendencies.

Growing and building a business isn't easy. Building and growing my business was a grueling, challenging, and significant risk. Yet, when the going got tough, I didn't back down. I didn't quit. Instead, I believed in myself, and through my stubbornness, tenacity, and ingenuity, I launched, built, and grew a multimillion-dollar business. Although certain aspects of starting my business were fun and exciting, there were moments when I was crippled by fear. But despite what I felt, I kept going, even when I was so scared to take another step. Don't get me wrong. I feared losing everything—reputation, money, and time that I could have used to climb the corporate ladder. What I eventually learned was to consistently take measured and calculated risks to limit the risks associated with every important decision.

I've discovered that every business owner is afraid of something. Understanding where that fear comes from could be the difference between those who grow exponentially and those who fail. Understanding your fears is the first step toward overcoming them in business and in life. The only time I hesitate in my business is when I'm either unsure of how to do something or when I'm afraid to take the action required. I've never let it stop me, however. As I gain a deeper understanding of each fear, I can cope more effectively. When I am afraid, I try to get specific and ask myself why I'm afraid. What is the cause? What is the absolute worst that can happen to me? Do I fear taking a risk or looking like a fool? Or am I afraid it will affect my family, friends, and relationships? The beginning phase of my entrepreneurship journey was the scariest and the most uncertain, and I feared most of my decisions would set me back financially and emotionally. All were viable concerns, but the one question I always ask when this occurs is, What is it I am most afraid will happen? When I answer this question truthfully, I often find that my fear is unfounded. Sometimes, the worst-case scenario you imagine is that you will succeed and there will be undesirable consequences of that success, such as being too busy, perceiving things differently, or having too many obligations. When this is the case, it might be beneficial to then look at the best-case scenario. Imagine how it would look if everything went according to plan. It must be perfect, not just right. Can this action you're afraid of bring positivity? Is it likely to have any impact on your future?

Face your fear head-on and deal with it. Find a strategy to eliminate a persistent fear that keeps coming up and blocking you from achieving your goals. For example, if your fear is based on a lack of knowledge, you can likely learn 95 percent of what you need to know by reading books by experts on the subject. A skill-based fear can easily be tackled as you engage in projects or acquiring skills necessary to operate your business, and once you do, it can and should eliminate any fear in the future. For instance, when the Home Shopping Network (HSN) informed me I needed to present my products on their channel, live, I panicked. I didn't know a single thing about media, let alone how to conduct my own shows on a major national shopping channel that reached millions of homes. I'm sure those executives at HSN didn't mean to terrify me, but they also informed me that all products and personalities are judged by their "sales dollars per minute" system. At that point, I felt there was at least a 50/50 chance I would fail miserably on national television. In order to cope with my fear, I conducted as much research as I could on the Internet about some of the most successful brands on television shopping channels. I watched as many video clips of their presentations as I could, and found some common threads between several brands. I also picked up a few tips on public speaking—what to say and how to say it. My first show was a smashing success. In fact, when I was told they were taking me off air forty minutes earlier than expected because everything sold out, I feared they were trying to be polite. I thought the real reason they took me off air was due to how horrible I must have sounded and how poor my sales must have been. Thank goodness I was wrong!

Another strategy for overcoming fear in business is recognizing that there will always be risks, and all you can do is minimize them the best you can.

Sadly, our fears often revolve around what people will think of us and our actions. Since this is the unfortunate reality, I ask myself what kind of person I prefer to be viewed as. Do I want to be seen as someone who is slightly foolish and takes careless actions even though they don't always work out? Or would I rather be remembered as someone who had many ideas but never acted on them? Naturally, it's the former I prefer.

Do not let fear prevent you from taking the next step toward your goal. This is the key. Author Mandy Hale, in her book *The Single Woman: Life, Love, and Dash of Sass*, wrote, "It's OKAY to be scared. Being scared means you're about to do something really brave."[3] Acknowledge you are afraid and do it anyway. Focus on the next step, the smaller goals, instead of the big project.

Despite everything I've learned in growing my business, the impactful truth is that the need to kick your fear in business never stops. As long as we continue to grow and stretch ourselves, fear will always be there. Fear is a sign that we're outside our comfort zones. With each action taken, however, your confidence grows, and that fear diminishes. In addition to reducing your fear in that particular situation, you strengthen your emotional and mental muscles to overcome fear in other areas of your life and business.

MANAGING YOUR FEAR

Even owners of billion-dollar corporations experience fear and anxiety about their businesses. Many CEOs agree that fear of failure is their leading cause of distress. In fact, most CEOs of large companies have more significant fears and stresses because the stakes are much higher. As an entrepreneur who started with very little money, I thought my fears would disappear after making a certain amount of money. But to my horror, my fears grew as my business grew. I had to overcome my fear of failure to achieve my ultimate goal of spending more time with my family without worrying about money.

How we approach our fears makes a difference. Henry Ford, the automaker and founder of the Ford Motor Company, is believed to have said, "Whether you think you can or think you can't, you're right." I believe this because many people quit before they even start a business. Why? Because taking the first step can be scary.

When I started my jewelry business, my family was nearly broke. Our family was growing, and I was petrified to take the leap. My father used to tell me to dream big because if you're willing to work for it and never give up, your dream will come true. I've had to adjust my goals out of fear several times and found my road to success was littered with wrong turns. However, each wrong turn led to discoveries and wisdom I would need down the road, all from getting past my uncertainty and fear. Getting past this fear of failure and an uncertain future was the blessing I needed to take my business to new heights.

Throughout my early days I combated fear by pausing, stepping back, and centering myself. Letting the problem present itself and viewing your situation objectively makes you more likely to see potential solutions. In business, things can move quickly. Identifying the problem is the first step toward changing it.

In dealing with my fear, I accepted that it is a natural human reaction. Whenever you feel fear, avoid judging it or yourself. Feeling shame only worsens the fear. Humans are naturally fearful creatures, so take time and remind yourself of that. Recognizing your fear as authentic and valid is the first step toward finding a solution.

Following the awareness of fear, pausing, literally pausing, is the critical next step. Good decisions cannot be made under duress or fear. Think of pausing a movie: all the characters freeze, everything stops moving, and you have time to observe. Taking a moment to pause creates space and time to breathe. You can pause for as long as you like—a minute, an hour, a day, or even longer. It's up to you. You may think, *But what if I need to respond right away? Can I pause if I don't have time?* In business you rarely get a do-over. It's always prudent to take the necessary time to digest and evaluate the various options before responding.

Whenever I face fears regarding business decisions, I stop and consider the worst potential consequence that could happen with my decision. In my business, those consequences could be losing a large purchase order, customer loss, or even loss of profits. Then, I ask myself what the exit strategy and backup plan is if the worst of my fears come true. And last, I ask if my decision will help me move toward my long-term goal. Over the years, I've come close to losing everything from purchase orders to important customers and even my entire company. But clarity and answers will come once you learn and adapt to analyzing your situation by pausing.

Next time you're afraid, whether about your business, your life, or the state of the world, be aware and manage your fear and uncertainty. We cannot control everything, we can only control how we respond to people and situations. But, even if you are afraid, you can implement strategies for taking the initiative to feel confident that you can manage whatever comes your way.

A quote often questionably attributed to Winston Churchill tells us that "success is not final, failure is not fatal: it is the courage to continue that counts." No matter who actually gave this advice, it holds true. So, gather your courage, get past your fear of failure, pause, gain clarity, and move yourself, your passion, and your business across the finish line.

KEY TAKEAWAYS

* Recognizing your fear as authentic and valid is the first step toward finding a solution in your business.

* Do not let fear prevent you from taking the next step toward your goal.

* The first step in understanding and kicking your fear is knowing what fears you will face when starting a new business.

* Wear the "expert" label, strive to be your best, and overcome the fear of impostor syndrome.

Ignite the Big Idea and Find Your Passion

If today were the last day of my life, would I want to do what I am about to do today? And whenever the answer has been "no" for too many days in a row, I know I need to change something.[1]

—STEVE JOBS

ANYONE WHO KNOWS ME UNDERSTANDS THAT I LOVE READING and writing and have invested considerable time and effort into both. I read fiction and nonfiction every day and read fifty to seventy-five books a year, depending on my schedule. Stephen King, in his book *On Writing: A Memoir of the Craft*, writes, "If you want to be a writer, you must do two things above all others: read a lot and write a lot. There's no way around these two things that I'm aware of, no shortcut."[2] My love of writing and reading remains strong, and I've written short stories, personal journals, and novels because I love the creativity it offers. Despite my passion for writing, many years passed before I ever considered publishing my work as a professional. However, I believe words can heal and change lives, and the healing power of words gave me the courage to pursue writing this book.

Along with writing, designing fresh and exciting jewelry expresses my emotions at the moment of creativity, and it is satisfying on all levels. Still, it took me years following the wrong passions and chasing money to find my true love and build a million-dollar business from it. I was lucky because many people never get to a place from which they can emotionally, mentally, and financially follow their dreams and passions. I'm convinced that if you have a deep passion, you must examine it thoroughly to understand if there is an opportunity to turn it into something profitable.

Confucius said, "Choose a job you love, and you'll never have to work a day in your life." The sentiment is worth exploring, even if the phrase itself could be argued. Acting on your passion should be your starting point if you want to do what you love. Passionate entrepreneurs are more likely to succeed than their less passionate peers, and there are many ways to turn your passion into a successful business. Whether you are considering starting a small business or changing careers, passion must play a crucial role. A strong work ethic, talent, ambition, intellect, discipline, persistence, and luck contribute to business and career success, but following your passion can make the most significant difference.

Your passion becomes an internal compass that helps you stay committed to achieving your vision, regardless of obstacles and challenges. Substantial research supports this theory. In 2019, a team of researchers led by Sylvia Hubner of the National University of Singapore designed a series of experiments to test the idea that entrepreneurial passion is predictive of organizational success. The researchers concluded,

> *We conceptualize entrepreneurial passion as an intense positive emotional experience felt by individuals engaging in entrepreneurial activities. Building on emotional contagion theory, we explain the contagion mechanism that determines*

how entrepreneurs' entrepreneurial passion stimulates an entrepreneurial passion response in employees, which in turn affects employee outcomes such as their commitment and work performance.[3]

Finding your true passion also means investing in your strengths and believing that your talents, skills, training, and experience will enable you to meet the goals necessary to achieve your vision. There is no room for doubt or second-guessing. Once you commit to the vision, your passion needs to be a raging fire in your belly that can provide powerful fuel for you on a long, arduous, nonlinear journey toward a successful business.

PASSION AND SUCCESS

We must first define what "success" means to understand passion and its significance. For some people, success means making large sums of money or achieving fame. Others believe success is the opportunity to align their passions with work while making a sustainable income, which is more important to them than big money or fame. The more money you make, the less value it has, making it hard to define success. Success means being proud of your accomplishments and being part of something that is meaningful to you. Following your passion also increases your chances of success because you put in time and effort with enthusiasm and zeal. Why is it critical to have passion for what you do? People are more resilient when confronted with obstacles if they are enthusiastic about their goals. Passionate people are more positive and capable of overcoming difficulties than those driven mainly by financial success. Likewise, the more passionate a person is about their work, the more likely they will work hard to improve their products, services, and, ultimately, themselves. The questions below will aid you in identifying your passion. Be honest as you answer them.

1. What do you like to do? What things do you dislike?

2. What are your strengths and weaknesses? What are you mediocre at, and what can you improve upon?

3. What did you love doing most as a child?

4. How can the activity from question #3 above be of service to others?

5. At least once or twice a day, picture yourself doing what you love as your full-time job. What does this look like?

Once you have answered these questions, it's time to evaluate how your passion can translate into a successful business. Consider these activities:

1. *Take inventory.* Write down your skills, gifts, and achievements, and internalize them with pride.

2. *Examine.* Probe your skills, gifts, and achievements to learn how they can help you enter a specific business market.

3. *Explore.* Find new opportunities that excite you and be open-minded about them.

4. *Write.* Scribble thoughts in your journal daily to find inspiration, problem-solve, and remind yourself of your passion.

5. *Network.* Seek like-minded people who will share your passion and provide useful advice, support, and encouragement.

Those with a clear idea of how they want to build their dream life are fortunate and should get started as soon as they feel comfortable with their plans. However, it is common for people to find passion after experiencing personal, even traumatic, challenges. This reminds me of my good friend, personal chef and TV show host, Daniel Green. As a child, Daniel grew up in a loving, middle-class family with no particular passion or interest until he struggled with weight in his late teens. In an effort to lose weight, he prepared healthy foods for himself. He experimented with various cuisines and invented hundreds of dishes. In addition to keeping his weight under control, he drastically improved his physical and mental health. Cooking is his passion, but sharing his amazing recipes is his greatest passion. He does not have a culinary degree or professional training in the culinary arts, but to date he has written and published thirteen cookbooks and conducted over ten thousand hours of live television shows. Through his passion, Daniel positively affected the lives of millions of people.

MAKE THE MOST OF YOUR STRENGTHS

Each of us has our own innate strengths. There are strengths you discover in times of crisis and others you discover as you progress through life. By applying your strengths, you discover what you are capable of and how to help others. Your newfound business will be much more satisfying if you do something you enjoy and are good at. I know this might seem far-fetched, but if you make the most of your strengths, leveraging them to your advantage, you will find they support and deliver a positive perspective leading you toward success. Remember, everything takes work. Very few people develop strengths without training and putting in their heart, soul, time, and effort. Skill requires training and cultivation. It takes intention, consistency, and passion. You might not find turning your passion into a successful business as daunting as you think. You can develop many skills, including soft skills like communication and leadership, so take advantage of your strengths to help you pursue your new passion. For example, your leadership skills will enable you to build an effective team, and your people skills will help you find funding.

LOOK BEFORE YOU LEAP

From the outside, all kinds of careers can seem glamorous, from show business to online sales, coaching, and even working in restaurants. Whatever your passion, find ways to gain an insider's perspective before you pursue it full time. After getting an inside look, if you find yourself just as passionate as before, you're on the right track. There are several ways in which you can get a taste of a different career without putting your current career at risk. You can volunteer and gain an insider's perspective while making valuable contacts or take on a part-time job in the field of your passion, which will allow you to make some extra money and gain valuable inside information.

BE GENUINELY PASSIONATE

The best way to get a fresh start is to find your passion and pursue it. People often go through their careers looking for new opportunities but are too afraid to leap. You need not suffer the same fate. Follow the money, but always follow your passion. Turning your passion into an exciting, thriving business is possible if you have the knowledge and dedication to see it through.

As an entrepreneur and business leader, I've learned there is a significant difference between having a vision for your business and being *passionate* about it. The overarching difference between the two is that the former is all about boldly gazing into the future—determining what is tangible and possible for you to achieve, even if it seems like a stretch. On the other hand, passion materializes when you believe with all your heart and soul in what you are doing or want to do, and you will do anything and everything you can to manifest your dream into reality.

Your primary *passion* may be identified, nurtured, and honed but cannot be pulled out of thin air. It must come from somewhere deep within you and be authentic to you. Most of us intuitively have an internal passion from an early age. Sometimes it dissipates and gets buried over the years, but it never entirely goes away. It's always there, ready to bubble up at the right time, such as when you have established a winning vision. For example, a love for jewelry-making may exist when you are a child working with beads. Over the years, that interest may fade as you move on to other things. Then, one day—as occurred in my case—circumstances arise to restimulate that feeling and make you realize you loved jewelry-making all along. It wasn't until that moment that you saw the potential for translating your passion for jewelry into a full-time, money-making career.

PASSION VERSUS MONEY

Do you have a great business idea you're passionate about? From here, getting a business off the ground requires gut-wrenching decisions. But what if pursuing your passion doesn't pay off? Every entrepreneur has asked this question. Parents, relatives, or even strangers may tell you to be realistic, don't work for yourself, find a job, stay there, be safe, and retire. On the other hand, friends and colleagues may tell you that following your passion is the only path to success. When pursuing your passion blindly, with little chance of earning money, it's natural to feel apprehensive, confused, and unsure.

Although we all need money to live, following your passions and desires leaves you with a sense of well-being and fulfillment that financial success alone just doesn't provide. This is about opportunity and the cards you've been dealt, but following one's passion seems more appealing than earning money. So, is there a fine line between pursuing a career you are passionate about and choosing a different or more financially rewarding one? It's all about pinpointing an alignment of passion with the marketplace.

METHOD TO DISCOVERING YOUR PASSION

Some people think they can start a business, even pursue success, without a single idea in their head. Most individuals do not know or understand precisely how to cultivate an idea from their passions. The key is identifying pertinent ideas and determining which one represents your passion and has some opportunity. Simply because it is your passion doesn't mean there is a market for it, or that you can build it into a business. There aren't any guarantees. The goal is to be knowledgeable about what other people need and want instead of focusing on what you want to sell them.

My father had a wicked sense of humor, which served him well, considering all he went through. Whenever I refused to do something or couldn't decide what to do, he would say, "You know what they say, one who chases two rabbits catches none. It's hard enough to catch a rabbit." As accurate as it may be, choosing only one option doesn't make it any easier.

Author Elizabeth Gilbert, in her book *Big Magic: Creative Living Beyond Fear*, wrote,

> *Passion can seem intimidatingly out of reach at times—a distant tower of flame, accessible only to geniuses and to those who are especially touched by God. But curiosity is a milder, quieter, more welcoming, and more democratic entity. The stakes of curiosity are also far lower than the stakes of passion. . . . Curiosity only ever asks one simple question: "Is there anything you're interested in?" Anything? Even a tiny bit? No matter how mundane or small? The answer need not set your life on fire or make you quit your job . . . it must capture your attention momentarily. But in that moment, if you can pause and identify even one tiny speck of interest in something, then curiosity will ask you to turn your head a quarter of an inch and look at the thing a little closer. Do it. It's a clue. It might seem like nothing, but it's a clue. Follow that clue. Trust it. See where curiosity will lead you next.*[4]

It is crucial to follow your passion. Still, combining your passion with selling your product for profit is complex, and it is nearly impossible to succeed in business without a profitable market in focus. Unfortunately, simply asking yourself what your passion is usually evokes responses that are too broad. Instead, it's best to ask yourself what your love is and what you are committed to. What is that one thing, more than anything else, you envision yourself doing for the rest of your life? By answering this question fully, you will be much closer to finding a profitable market niche because passion, product, and profit don't always intersect easily. The process can be elusive and frustrating, but it is not impossible. It is possible to discover a profitable product offering by following specific steps. So, when searching for the one primo passion that drives you, here are factors to consider and ask yourself:

1. What are you most passionate about?

2. Do you have knowledge or skills in one particular area?

3. Who is your ideal customer?

4. How easily can you attract your ideal customer?

5. How much income can you earn in the first year?

6. How does your idea align with your life's mission?

IDENTIFYING YOUR PASSIONS AND COMMITMENTS
On a sheet of paper, list ten things you're passionate about. They need not be arranged in any particular order. If you feel stuck during this time of self-reflection, write down any complaints about things in your life that could be improved. There is usually a passion or commitment behind complaints.

Next, continue your list by adding your expertise or features of products you intend to develop that benefit the end user and customer. Once you have this list, brainstorm and research varying markets for your product or service, then list all the people and circumstances from which your product or service might benefit.

It isn't enough to just identify a market and a product or service. Profit potential must be thoroughly researched. Several marketers recommend finding an empty niche where you can dominate the market. If you have a large marketing budget, that's great. Find niches where people are already buying. You can use many tools to research and find products and services that are highly profitable and in high demand, such as:

- Google Search
- Google AdWords
- Google Trends
- Amazon Keywords and Strings of Phrases

Google Search
To begin your search, use the items or words you listed as features, areas of knowledge, or specific target markets. Then note how many Google ads there are for this topic area. For example, many sponsored ads indicate that people are successfully selling products. Click on the ads to see what people sell and how much they charge.

Google AdWords
Search Google's keyword tool for phrasing ideas about your product or the problem your customer is having, which they might enter into Google to find a solution. Ignore the number of hits. Instead, consider the phrasing people use instead to search for information.

Google Trends
Google Trends allows you to compare keywords or phrases to see which option is searched more often. One aspect of Google Trends that sets it apart from other Google offerings is that it breaks down phrases and keywords from different regions around

the globe. Google Trends is a great tool to find what ideas and concepts would potentially make a great business idea. For example, I went to Google Trends to test the waters and typed "How to make more money." It got a decent response, but when I typed in "How to start a business," it got a slightly better hit rate. Then, diving deeper, I searched "How to start a luxury jewelry business," and it showed a much better response. Use this tool and explore the possibilities.

Amazon Keywords and Strings of Phrases
Often overlooked as a product or service search criteria, the goldmine for market research is Amazon.com. First, check out the best-selling books on your topic. It's a good sign if there are tons of entries. Next, look at the top sellers and see what makes them so appealing to so many people. Then, refine your ideas further using the information you've gained from your searches. Next, cross-reference your brainstorming list for innovative ideas that stick out to you. Finally, consider what's being offered in these markets and what's missing so you can add new value to a market that already buys these products.

NEVER GIVE UP
Warren Buffett, also known as the Oracle of Omaha, said, "Never give up searching for the job that you are passionate about."[5] I have never considered giving up on finding my passion, and neither should you. As a way to demonstrate my passion for pursuing the best opportunity, I measured each of my three major passions using the exact details, such as market, level of interest, goals, target audience, and earning and income potential. Based on these five factors, I developed a system that ranks each option from 1 to 5, with 5 being the most ideal. Follow my example and use the same steps and techniques to discover your passion. It is critical to be honest with yourself because a wrong decision can lead to lost time, energy, and financial peril.

To help you determine which idea represents your best opportunity, ask yourself why people would care about your idea. To be successful in business, you need as many people to be interested in your idea as possible. To determine whether your business is sustainable and long-lasting, ask yourself the following questions:

- Is the idea going to solve a problem for a large enough group of people?
- Will the idea save people time or money?
- Does the idea inspire people?
- How does the idea impact other people's well-being?
- Can the idea help heal, change a life, or create a movement?
- Does the idea raise awareness or educate about something?

I have loved jewelry for as long as I can remember. Even as a young girl, I loved how my mother cherished her exquisite jewelry collection. She kept her pieces in an ornate mahogany jewelry box carved with ancient symbols and told my siblings and me the stories behind each piece. Even though I loved jewelry, I was unsure about starting a business to sell my designs. However, after asking myself the questions listed above, I realized that many people love jewelry and wear it for important occasions in their lives—weddings, birthdays, anniversaries, graduations, holidays, and so on. Through research, I had discovered that there was not a large number of unique styles on the market. Unfortunately, a few large manufacturers controlled the distribution to retailers, resulting in similar styles that looked dated and rarely reflected individual personality. It was difficult for buyers to find unique jewelry that catered to them at a price they could afford. If I could come up with a unique and special collection, keep it affordable without sacrificing quality, I could solve that problem for many people. I found my niche through discovery and self-assessment.

Now that I knew *what* I wanted to do, I had to figure out if it was the right path for me. What about my other passions? To decide if this was the path on which I would enter the world of entrepreneurship, I developed a rating system to help me consider the options I had. My system was based on my passions and skills/ expertise, income potential within the first two years, ease of finding customers in the first year, and alignment with my ultimate life goal of those passions.

Using my ranking system, I selected fiction writer, jewelry designer, and freelance graphic designer as my top three passions. While my skills and expertise on fiction writing were so-so, I ranked that category at a 3 because I lacked confidence in my writing skills. Even though writing is a tremendous creative expression, as far as income potential, I gave it a ranking of a 1 because it would have taken two years or more before I could turn a profit, if I was lucky. While being a fiction writer was one of my ultimate goals, I'd rank it a 4 because attracting a loyal fan base as a writer isn't easy. I ranked the ease of attracting ideal customers a 2, giving me a grand total of 10. Freelance graphic designer scored even lower. However, my rankings for jewelry designer were as follows: my passion and skills came in at 5 each, potential for high income ranked 3, and ease of attracting ideal customers was a 4, totaling a winning score of 17 out of 20.

So, following my passion, I started a small jewelry company and grew it into a multimillion-dollar business. Not a day goes by that I'm not thankful for making the right decision. You can do the same. You will succeed by following your heart's sincere desire and aligning the details of a market and potential target customer base with your passion.

While it's possible to develop a profitable product for a profitable market niche within minutes, it might take a little more effort than you expected. Invest some time in researching and evaluating each of your ideas. Of course, finding the intersection of what you love to do and a profitable market need is ideal, but being fully engaged in what you love most will bring you and your customers more joy and satisfaction. Steve Jobs said it the best when he spoke to graduates at Stanford University in 2005, saying, "For the past thirty-three years, I have looked in the mirror every morning and asked myself: 'If today were the last day of my life, would I want to do what I am about to do today?' And whenever the answer has been 'No' for too many days in a row, I know I need to change something."[6]

Your work will fill a large part of your life, and the only way to be truly satisfied is to do what you believe is great work. And the only way to do great work is to love what you do. So, if you haven't found it yet, keep looking. Don't settle. As with all matters of the heart, you'll know when you find it.

KEY TAKEAWAYS

- Passion must be considered when starting a business or changing careers.
- Success depends on strong values, talent, intellect, persistence, and luck, but following your passion can make all the difference.
- Planning is essential to launching your passion project.
- Matching your passion to a market need or problem is vital to getting a project off the ground.

CHAPTER 4

Targeting Your Audience

Perfection is not attainable, but if we chase perfection, we can catch excellence.[1]

—VINCE LOMBARDI

WHEN I STARTED MY BUSINESS, I WAS EXCITED BEYOND MEASURE and believed everyone wanted and needed jewelry. In my mind, I had a worldwide audience, it was a no-brainer, and I'd be a momentous success. Yet, I was wrong. I quickly realized that targeting everyone successfully was an impossible task. Millions of people wear jewelry, but much of the jewelry on the market is expensive, hard to find, and tailored to the well-off. But I soon discovered an enormous gap between exquisitely elegant high-priced jewelry and the cheap, knock-off market. So, I studied the market and focused on narrowing my niche, which targeted an audience of individuals who wanted uniquely designed, top-quality jewelry at affordable prices.

I targeted professional women who worked outside the home. In 1989, the jewelry market was saturated with fancy diamond jewelry considered too ostentatious for a professional working environment. Meanwhile, cheap costume jewelry made of plastic, alternative metals, and glued stones was not desirable to wear to

33

work. Once I focused on finding my market, I hit the ground running, using my market as my foundational engine to build my business. Targeting a small niche within the jewelry market made everything easier. I focused on unique workplace-friendly designs, marketing messages that addressed the needs of professional working women, and price points that were budget-friendly.

Targeting your audience and market for your product and business isn't for the faint of heart, and it will take effort and substantial due diligence. It will take experimentation, even failure, to find the right path. In growing your business, you will fail more than once. It is often said that a person who never makes a mistake never tries anything new. You will make mistakes as you progress, but defining your target audience and the market is an important step. It is at the heart of everything you do to ensure your business's longevity and success.

Many entrepreneurs define their target audience too broadly, much like I did at first. You can't be everything to everyone, and when I ask people about their target audience, the reply is often, "Everyone loves it, and my product and service are perfect for everyone." That is a red flag. However, when I ask budding entrepreneurs to be more specific about their market, I am often met with resistance and confusion, and it does not take long for them to sound lost. This makes sense: when you believe in a product, you want the whole world to know about it. Many potential customers are out there, and you don't want to ignore them. So, I understand why new business owners don't want to narrow their target audience. Let me explain the reasons why they should.

The experience of owning a business is both exciting and frustrating. There may come a time when a business doesn't flow as quickly as you'd like, whether you've recently taken the plunge into business ownership or are an experienced entrepreneur. Where do you go from here? It's time to spend money on marketing and advertising to fill your sales funnel with leads. When deciding who your target audience is, it is important to understand that not everyone is your customer. You can achieve a higher return on investment (ROI) by clearly defining your target audience. You may believe you have an exceptional product or service, with many people interested in what you offer. Good for you, and no one wants to stop you from selling to them if they knock on your door. Yet you cannot pursue everyone with every marketing campaign you launch. You do not want to waste valuable dollars on ineffective marketing that hits the wrong market sector. Take your time exploring your options, brainstorming, and dividing your target market into subsets to create targeted marketing campaigns.

You Might Not be the Best at Everything

Speed and convenience are important to some people, quality is essential to others, and some are simply looking for the cheapest option. There's no way you can always be the best at everything. Choose a race you can win, and address those who care about it while ignoring the rest. Whenever it comes to business, one rule that always applies is that not all people are equal in value. Some people buy quickly, often, and a lot, while others don't. And it's not that your product or service is terrible, it's just that they may not be looking for what you offer. Some people will get a great deal of value from your product, while others will require a lot of follow-up and support. Who do you want to talk to first? Owning a business is challenging, especially when starting, because every person you reach and try to reach costs money. Marketing costs can be astronomical, but you must spend money to capture people's attention, even if you don't sell anything to them.

Knowing the probable expense, ask yourself, *How much is it worth paying for someone's attention?* For instance, after I had some success reaching the duty-free market, I decided to contact United Airlines' inflight duty-free program. To participate, it was necessary for me to fly to Chicago to meet with their buyers several times a year, an approximate cost of $6,000 per year. It took a couple of years to obtain my first purchase order, but when it finally came, it was well over $300,000. While the $12,000 I spent on that account was worth the effort, I would have had second thoughts about spending similar amounts of money, time, or effort on a lesser-quality account with much less profit/revenue potential.

There can, and usually will be, more than one target audience, even though you may have varying markets and audiences. Men and women looking for expensive, fancy diamond jewelry were markets under my umbrella with different needs that had to be approached differently. Your message becomes diluted and confused if you try to target different audiences with the same approach. The more you dilute your message, the less likely your audience will read and act on it. The more specific your definition of your target audience, the more refined your message will be. While you are trying to figure out which market segment will be most profitable, expanding into new segments, or attracting clients, customers, and possibly investors, you may likely consider more than one audience at a time. But it's important to note that you should not group them all together. You cannot automatically copy and paste the same approach from one audience to another, even if some parts of your communication are the same. For each audience, you must consider the message, the media, and the tactics separately and invest time, money, and planning. By being patient and focusing your efforts where the opportunity is greatest, you will gradually get to where you want to go.

Today, the smaller your niche and the more specific your target market, the better your odds are in growing your business. Your ability to develop specific products and create marketing messages that connect you emotionally with your target audience becomes much easier after correctly identifying your niche. In my business, after I identified the large group of professional women who worked outside the home, I developed a high-quality jewelry collection with an understated elegance that exuded the aura of success. My marketing message became super simple. It went something like this: "Are you looking for high-quality, elegant jewelry to wear to work or a special occasion confidently?"

This reminds me of my friend, Daniel Green, who specializes in delicious, healthy options designed for moms who constantly juggle the needs of their work and family. In a recent conversation with Daniel, he explained that he ensures his recipes can be easily made with common, everyday ingredients so that a busy mom wouldn't need to go shopping for several exotic ingredients before she starts cooking. As an example, instead of using a tablespoon of fermented soybeans, he suggests soy sauce and a few other healthy options that can be substituted with common ingredients found in most kitchens in America. I can easily understand why Daniel has a cult-like following.

Defining your niche is important. You must determine details about your ideal customer, for example, age range, gender, favorite TV shows, interests, average household income, where they shop and work, and so on. You can develop better products and generate more profits if you know your ideal customer. Knowing your customer allows you to tailor your branding message. Trying to do too much for too many people is a mistake often made by new business owners. Doing one thing better than anyone else and offering it to many people for higher sales will lead, eventually, to larger profits.

In business school, I was taught to define a target market precisely, but I did not initially apply it to my business. I thought, *Who wouldn't love premium quality jewelry with fabulous designs?* Although many people love beautiful jewelry, I learned it was impossible to market to every market segment. It was a hard lesson to learn, but the numbers supported it. I had to choose. Initially, I defined my target market as college-educated women aged twenty-one to sixty-five looking for jewelry to wear to work, older women who love jewelry for social status, and men who buy jewelry as gifts. I was under the grand illusion that my passion and jewelry were perfect for everyone and that everyone was my target audience.

I was wrong, and it was a costly mistake.

I believe jewelry is typically purchased to celebrate milestones and passed down from generation to generation. I was determined to ensure everyone could access the highest quality jewelry at affordable prices. I passionately believed I was right about my target market, and I worked tirelessly to attract as many customers as possible, spending excessive amounts of time and financial resources researching magazine editors, executives at department stores, and buyers, as well as working with local department stores for dedicated events and trunk shows. I worked as hard as possible, but were things booming? Did I get sales from men looking to surprise their wives, mothers, or daughters with beautiful jewelry? Of course I did, but the sales did not justify the effort and cost. Even though I generated sales from trunk shows and made some headway in department stores, the hours were demanding as I struggled to keep up with designing exclusive collections for specialty jewelry stores, department stores, and my one-of-a-kind customers. Plus, I was responsible for my fledgling company's accounting, marketing, quality control, importing, shipping, and receiving. While my engines were burning overtime with my passion, I soon discovered this wasn't sustainable. I was burned out, exhausted, and needed to reassess my efforts to address my time and financial resources to increase my ROI.

I paused and assessed where my business was and where it was heading. Then, I narrowed my focus and targeted professional women between the ages of thirty and sixty-five. I didn't forget men, children, and other women, but I narrowed my market to a specific demographic and class: professional women. Many women of this stature, demographic, and class were looking for ways to stand out in their workplace as someone who takes care of herself and exudes success. I catered to their needs by creating jewelry that complemented their polished look.

With my newfound product development streamlined, I was able to focus on the unique types of jewelry this group needed. Now with my focus targeted, my marketing amplified and simplified, and my passion and clarity at an all-time high, I communicated with my ideal customers more effectively, speaking to how they could look polished, successful, and confident with the right amount of sparkle. This move proved to be a huge success.

It was a risky move and took guts, but even though I had a minor drop in sales after I stopped marketing to high-income individuals and reduced my efforts with small, independent jewelry stores around the country, I built a meaningful customer base, a formidable reputation as a jewelry designer for modern women, and a premium, niche brand by focusing on that specific group of women.

EVOLUTIONARY OR REVOLUTIONARY?

Do you have an evolutionary or revolutionary product? Is your product one-of-a-kind or an improved version of something that already exists? There are no right or wrong answers to this question. Revolutionary products are new and unfounded ideas never before seen or introduced to the marketplace. Evolutionary products improve upon something that already exists, making them bigger, better, or even faster, whether through new technology or new materials. It is common for someone to tweak, bend, and pivot an old business model to take it in a new direction. Once you have your product or service idea in front of you, if you find other potential competitors already on the market, that's actually excellent news because it indicates the demand for your type of product. Differentiating your product from all others on the market will be one of your significant challenges. To do this, you must extensively research your market in the initial stages of your business journey, gathering relevant information about comparable products.

There are two distinct ways for any product or service to succeed. The first is evolutionary: offering something that is already used by a large population segment but finding a way to produce it cheaper or faster, or in a way that substantially improves the product and the customer experience. For example, Americans love hamburgers, and burgers are now a staple on nearly every restaurant menu. McDonald's entered this incredibly crowded market with its quick and affordable burgers and became one of the world's most successful fast-food companies. On the surface, it sounds simple, but the founders overcame many failures, setbacks, and challenges to excel at consistently delivering tasty burgers cheaper and faster than anyone else on the market.

Another example is the story of Starbucks. Like McDonald's, Starbucks also took a high-demand product and entered one of the most crowded markets in the industry. However, Starbucks took the opposite direction from McDonald's, improving the products and elevating the customer experience by offering a formidable menu of customizable choices one cup at a time at a higher price.

The second way for a product or service to succeed is to do something revolutionary: inventing a product or service no one has ever offered before. It is believed that Leonardo DaVinci once said, "It had long come to my attention that people of accomplishment rarely sat back and let things happen to them. They went out and happened to things." Suppose your research shows there is nothing like your product on the market. This could be fantastic news in that there wouldn't be a lot of competition, but it could also point to no interest by consumers and little or no demand for such products. It could also mean the demand for the product is high, but so is the cost of manufacturing it. This is known as a *barrier to entry*, a business term describing the factors that can prevent newcomers from entering a market. This reminds me of my friend Vince, a professionally trained chef. Vince dreamed of offering consumers a line of premade sauces using only the freshest, organic, non-GMO ingredients. Throughout his thirty-plus-year career as an executive chef at various hotels worldwide, he became passionate about international cuisine. His vision was to introduce international cooking, such as Mexican, Korean, Vietnamese, French, and Japanese, to American consumers. He insisted on offering his products at an affordable price without sacrificing authentic taste or quality. He invested a lot of time and money perfecting his sauces for consistency and taste, but eventually found that while they were amazing, he couldn't mass produce them at a reasonable cost. He could have used lesser-quality ingredients, but then his company would never have gained traction with his target audience. If you don't see comparable products on the market, stop and assess why that is. Do your due diligence to avoid potential pitfalls.

Suppose you are indeed the first to offer a revolutionary product. You may be in a perfect position to solve problems, improve lives, or even affect positive change worldwide. An example of a revolutionary product that solved serious problems and improved lives was a pump invented in 1949 by Candido Jacuzzi, a father who wanted to help his toddler Kenneth, who suffered from rheumatoid arthritis, by offering the benefits of hydrotherapy in the comfort of his own home. Prior to his invention, Jacuzzi would have to take his son to communal facilities that offered hydrotherapy. Jacuzzi's pump could be used in residential bathtubs, eliminating the need to travel. Of all the stories I researched, I chose this story as case study material because I love the origin of his invention, his love for his son, and his passion for his work. At the time of his invention, the natural demand for this product was deficient, and the easiest thing would have been to move on to something else. But Jacuzzi didn't stop there. Throughout his extensive career, spanning several decades, Jacuzzi obtained fifty patents, a formidable barrier to entry into his particular industry. His dedication to his passion and son was nothing short of remarkable.

Jacuzzi's experience is a perfect demonstration of how, when you are the first to offer a product, you must find an effective way to educate the public about its features, benefits, and why they need it, which can cost years of time and lots of money. Can you imagine the uphill battle Jacuzzi fought convincing bathtub manufacturers to invest money and time to incorporate his new invention with no apparent demand? Additionally, even if some manufacturers wanted to try, they would have had to overcome challenges with potential product liability and production issues. Despite spending hundreds of thousands of dollars on over fifty patents, Jacuzzi faced tremendous adversity before his product became a household name. This lesson applies to you. Take your passion and protect it, push it, and allow no one or anything to stop you from bringing it to the market and achieving success.

TARGET AUDIENCE TYPES
The first step toward designing your market plan is to understand the types of target audiences. It is common for target audiences to be broad and diverse, and you can effectively communicate with your potential customers by targeting multiple audiences. Explore the attributes of distinct target audiences by discovering what works best for your business model.

Purchase Intention
A customer's purchase intent is their likelihood of purchasing a particular product. Small and large businesses can narrow their target audience based on purchase intent. However, the best way to create advertising tailored to each product is to target audiences looking to purchase precisely what you're offering.

Interests
Interests, such as hobbies, can also help business owners target audiences. Like purchase intent, interests indicate the products and advertisements to which potential customers will be drawn.

Customers who see ads aligned with their interests will immediately feel more connected to that product, which leads to prominent sales.

Subcultures

Subcultures are groups of people who share common beliefs and behaviors. Subcultures are more specific than interests and can involve belief systems, fashion, and genres of music and art. There are many subcultures that people can belong to and many overlap. For example, a person can identify herself as a proud hippie, enjoy surfing, and love wearing luxurious, unique jewelry.

My jewelry company had different audiences: men, women who sought jewelry to wear to work, and women who sought luxury jewelry for special occasions and events. Many identified themselves as hippies, flower children, hipsters. Once I categorized those audiences with different needs, I was able to create and market collections of floral jewelry for women who identified themselves as "flower children" and a collection of retro-styled jewelry for those who identified themselves as "hipsters."

Demographics

A demographic profile of a target audience provides information about a particular group of users, visitors, and customers. Using demographics, we can break up a large number of people and group them based on their characteristics. In the business world, the following demographics are common:

- Income
- Gender
- Age
- Education
- Economic Status and Profile
- Family Cycle

- Interests and Hobbies
- Spending Patterns

Businesses use target audience demographics to hone in on their target market. So it would be best to create different identifiers to determine who would benefit most from your products or services.

Super Cultures
The concept of super cultures refers to a collection of cultures and subcultures that interact, share similar features, and have a sense of unity as a group. Super cultures are comprised of elements from several subcultures that span multiple demographics. Brainstorm and research your market to verify and list the different super cultures for your product or service.

DETERMINING YOUR BUSINESS'S CUSTOMERS
Earlier, I stated you can't be everything to everyone in your business. If you try to do so, your marketing will be weak and miss the mark, and the goal is to ensure your marketing efforts stand out from that of your competitors. Throughout history, even conglomerate companies and advertisers have spent millions of dollars trying to figure out how to stay on top of consumer trends. As an example, let's look at the famous Super Bowl commercials. Many Super Bowl advertisers have discovered and perfected the formula for reaching the right customers. The commercials are a mix of humor and realism. Selling a product or service depends on marketing that sells emotion, and one of the greatest examples is the 2015 Nationwide Insurance commercial that featured a boy "talking about all the things he won't be able to do in life . . . because he's dead."[2] The commercial was profoundly influential, even in front of a football-loving, pizza, wings, and beer fanatics audience, because of the profoundly moving message that hit home with millions. Amid fun and games, Nationwide's move

was brilliant, as the commercial hit viewers from the blind side, portraying a young boy who fell victim to an accident and died. Nationwide took only forty-eight seconds to deliver the unbridled shock. Yet that shock morphed into sales, a prime example of the enduring power of something so damning, controversial, and memorable. Nationwide's roll of the dice and gamble paid off, hitting an emotional nerve across many potential and diverse groups of customers.

This is what you must do with your marketing. Hit a nerve, evoke emotion, portray the need, show the desire, and do your best to pinpoint the exact customers that would benefit from your product or service without beating them over the head. So, as you do your due diligence on your potential customers, consider these four types:

1. Prospective Customers

2. Ideal Customers

3. Interested Customers

4. Untargeted Customers

Prospective Customers
You can serve this group and enjoy doing so, but you don't want to define all your advertisements around them. This type of customer would be one who might use your product or service only occasionally but still benefit from it.

Ideal Customers
These are the perfect customers for your product or service. These clients would raise their hand loud and clear, wanting your product or service, and are straightforward with their needs and desires to own it. It may take an immense effort to locate and market to your ideal customer, but once you figure out the message

(remember Nationwide's commercial), your marketing will be effective in reaching them.

Interested Customers

Although this client has good margins and is a good fit, they are not the ideal client. These companies or individual customers can afford your product or service but would not buy as often to sustain your business.

Untargeted Customers

You cannot or do not want to serve this group. It is still possible for them to do business with you, but you do not want to concentrate too much on acquiring their business.

IDENTIFYING YOUR CUSTOMERS

At this stage, you may wonder how you identify different types of customers. I have developed a three-tiered approach that I've found effective.

Customers likely to provide the highest margin for your business are not bargain shoppers who only buy items that are on sale. These confident customers with high margins generate the most profit for you. Airlines are exceptionally good at figuring out their high-profit margin customers. On a typical flight from Los Angeles to New York, the airline will collect more than twenty diverse types of fares, ranging from super bargain fares as low as $150, to $3,200 for a fully refundable first-class ticket, depending on the customer's value system for convenience, such as legroom, and the overall flight experience. A significant percentage of our custom-design engagement ring customers at one of my companies, Rachel & Victoria, gladly pay extra for original designs, such as design fees, cad-cam drawings, and original mold fees, in addition to the manufacturing fees. Find out if you have a segment of customers willing to pay more for an elevated product, service, or experience in your business.

Next, you need to evaluate whether you will have enough of these customers to sustain your business. Conduct market research by looking at past sales data to identify if this customer base is large enough.

It's also good practice to examine your competitors' products and services and determine how yours is superior. How is your selling proposition unique? Are your products and services of the highest quality? Make sure your marketing content educates your ideal client on how you can help them. Identifying your ideal client will increase the ROI from your marketing efforts.

Transforming your idea into a business involves all these steps and an intensive approach to exposing your product or service to specified masses. It's important to develop a marketing plan *before* you launch, whether promoting your product to specific online communities or advertising to drive traffic to your website or brick-and-mortar store. A successful marketing plan typically includes public relations outreach to media, social media promotions, word of mouth, and influencer marketing. Then, once you're off the ground, use the momentum to build your business. Think big about your brand and put everything into action to scale it into a million-dollar business.

POSITIVITY IS KEY

It is said that misery loves company, so ensure there is no misery in your new business. Doubt and fear will only prevent you from taking the necessary risks. People will inevitably question your ideas and business, but if they don't believe you can overcome them, they will perpetuate their negativity toward you. It is easier to deal with mistakes or obstacles if you stay positive above the negative because you will face both as a new business owner. Success isn't guaranteed. It's all about adapting your idea and seeing what works. And when you don't succeed at one thing, keep trying and adapting until you reach the pinnacle of success.

Key Takeaways

- Transforming your idea into a business involves several steps and an intensive approach to exposing your product or service to the specified masses.

- Today, the smaller your niche and more specific your target market, the better your odds are in growing your business.

- Owning a business is challenging, especially when starting.

- Marketing can be an astronomical expense because every person you reach and try to reach costs money, but you must spend money wisely to capture people's attention.

- With your marketing, you must hit a nerve, evoke emotion, portray the need, show the desire, do your best to pinpoint the exact customer base that would benefit from your product or service without beating them over the head.

- If there aren't any products like yours in the market, be aware of other barriers to entry, such as high production costs and potential lack of demand.

CHAPTER 5

The Essential Five Cs to Success

*Sometimes, when we want something so badly, we fear failure
more than we fear being without that thing.*[1]
—MATTHEW J. KIRBY

WHEN MY FAMILY LIVED IN KOREA, WE HAD A COMFORTABLE
life and were well-off, but my father wanted a brighter future
and dreamed of taking us all to the United States. The move was
needed; South Korea was ruled by a military junta and our future
seemed quite uncertain, especially for a family with four daughters. Even though the desire to leave Korea was strong, it took
years for my parents to finally generate the courage to apply for a
visa. However, once we crossed the ocean, it only took a few days
to discover that the Korean government had wiped out all our
family's assets and savings. Our struggles became the nightmare
we feared. With only thirty dollars to their name, my parents
tried to be stoic and brave. I knew the situation was dire. We were
broke, had nothing to eat, and no place to live; the pressure and
hopelessness filled my parents' eyes and lined their tired faces. But,
as any parent would, they worried and wavered about returning to
Korea, especially my mother. She was scared and believed there

was still time, a chance to reclaim our home and property, put my sisters and me back in school, and reestablish our lives.

As the oldest child, I had to be brave, but I was scared and desperately hoped everything would improve. However, my father, a man of determination and commitment, insisted that every reason we left Korea would still be waiting for us if we returned. I admired him. He stood bravely, telling us that our family had to commit to making a new life. We couldn't go back, and there was no choice but to stick with our vision, ride it out, move forward, and make a new life. My father's steadfast commitment to providing a better future for his family never wavered. His deep strength and commitment to his vision made me realize we must remain committed to our dreams and passion. Just like making a new life, being an entrepreneur and moving toward a million-dollar business requires a strong commitment to the cause. It takes what I call the "Five Cs of Entrepreneurship":

1. Commitment

2. Courage

3. Confidence

4. Curiosity

5. Character

COMMITMENT
Commitment is what turns a promise into reality and ensures your intentions are boldly expressed. Words are not enough; actions speak louder. Commitment means making time when there is none, coming through time after time, year after year. An individual's character is shaped by their commitment, their ability to change forces, and their daily triumph over skepticism. This rings true within every entrepreneurial process, where the founder transforms and leads the cause, remaining at the center

of opportunity-seeking, starting and creating new products or services, leading, solving problems, and motivating the mission and vision. Like my father, I believe that human spirit, energy, behavior, drive, and commitment create businesses' greatest ideas and attributes. I believe it is critical to adapt these traits to your life. Unfortunately, many will fail or underperform due to lack of commitment to their goals. What it takes is a brilliant aptitude, with the difference being an invisible and intangible trait involving tenacity, commitment, and, most of all, grit and determination. It is not for the faint of the heart.

As an entrepreneurial leader, commitment to the vision must be nurtured and maintained for the long haul once you've clarified your business idea and goals. While many people are passionate about their business or interest, you can fall victim to quitting without a firm commitment to the venture when things get tough. Unfortunately, according to an article in *Inc.* magazine titled "7 Reasons Why People Give Up on Their Goals Too Early," many people give up on their goals too early when the goal seems too challenging for a variety of reasons.[2] Others are influenced by those who have overcome more difficult challenges and never give up.

Commitment and determination are more important than any other factor when it comes to success in business. These two traits make an entrepreneur capable of overcoming incredible obstacles and compensating for other weaknesses. In the beginning stages of growing their business, most entrepreneurs are under constant pressure in regard to their time, emotions, patience, and loyalty. They are often asked to make sacrifices, and their desire to succeed must equal their refusal to give up. Many entrepreneurs desire success, but only a few have the perseverance and dogged tenacity to achieve it. Commitment, as a trait, can be instilled, but as a leading entrepreneur, committing and knowing when to walk away is also necessary for success. As a new business owner, you must be realistic about what is not working and being open to possibilities. You must depend on your courage and fortitude to solve major problems, working around an issue to find the solution.

Courage

According to *Merriam-Webster's Dictionary*, courage is the "mental or moral strength to venture, persevere, and withstand danger, fear, or difficulty."[3] When we think of great leadership and entrepreneurship, we imagine someone who emanates strength and confidence. Entrepreneurs often believe that to lead their companies they must present themselves as fearless and self-assured. However, the best leaders keep going even when they're not confident, revealing to their teams openly that they don't know what to do but assuring them they will figure it out. It's all about courage.

Business schools teach that if everyone had unlimited time and the same information, they would make the right decision. Yet, in the real world, business owners must make decisions in real time, often without all the necessary information, because indecision could result in a loss of opportunity, competitive disadvantage, or immediate income loss. As an entrepreneur and new business owner, making tough decisions requires wisdom and courage on a daily basis. When we defeat our fears, we gain courage. And unlike courage, fear is an instinctive trait, an awareness of danger, and an emotional state of mind that can be overcome. Fear is natural to humans, but courage is something that we must learn.

History's greatest leaders have publicly committed to things they didn't know how to accomplish. For example, the newly elected president of the United States, John F. Kennedy, announced in 1960 that the country would put a man on the moon within a decade. It took courage to make that enormous commitment to the American people and the world. Although the United States did not have the capability at the time to send a man to the moon, Kennedy committed to making it happen. While making a promise like this could have been disastrous for Kennedy, it turned out to be a success. Likewise, great entrepreneurs risk their reputations to move forward with big goals. When their ambitions are not yet attainable, their vision and innovation drive them forward. Doing so takes the initial courage to be willing to deal with challenges as well as long-term courage to continually take calculated and weighted risks to move the needle forward.

CONFIDENCE

Confidence is derived from preparation and an understanding of the direction you intend to take your business. You can become a better entrepreneur, be happier, and increase your chances of success if you focus on one factor—your confidence. Starting out as an entrepreneur, you may be too self-conscious to tell people about your business. Building confidence is crucial to your mental and emotional well-being and success as an entrepreneur. Instilling strong confidence in yourself and standing firm in your decisions will boost your self-esteem. Some people will try to undercut your confidence, but your goal is to build it through strategy, systematizing, and successes; even small successes are confidence-building. Lack of confidence can lead to self-doubt and fear, and some may even develop impostor syndrome. But if you strive to build more confidence, you can better cope with the mental stress and understand yourself as a leader. You can increase your capabilities over time, and confident leaders can implement and should possess a positive sense of self-worth and the ability to bounce back after failure.

Confidence is a positive attribute that must be present to build your business. However, there must be a balance between being confident and being overconfident. You can hurt yourself if you have too much confidence, especially if the experience does not match your expertise or talent. But a lack of confidence can harm your chances of success as well. To reach the level of success you envision, a personally developed system must maintain a balance of confidence. Overconfident individuals have ruined projects with enormous potential by dismissing valuable advice from knowledgeable colleagues. Many passionate, talented individuals do not make a difference with their expertise because they lack the confidence.

The more you build confidence, the more you accomplish, and the better and stronger you feel, making yourself more successful. Prominent levels of balanced confidence bring more opportunities, teach persistence, and make it easier to overcome obstacles. Self-confidence comes from trusting your abilities, choices, and values. A positive self-perception comes from within yourself—from an inner understanding of your strengths and weaknesses.

A lack of self-confidence can make building, growing, and managing your own business difficult. My practical advice for building confidence is to remind yourself how far you've come, consider the small or big obstacles you've overcome, and reflect by writing down the positive reasons that others, such as customers, employees, and investors, should believe in you and your product. If you don't believe in yourself, no one else will. So, a system, such as keeping a daily journal that reaffirms why you should believe in yourself, will help build confidence. Self-confidence grows once you begin the cycle. As you follow your vision for a million-dollar business, build self-confidence by celebrating wins, even the small ones, and accept praise from others while delivering positive affirmations to others. Be humble but steadfast by identifying your strengths and weaknesses, and stop comparing yourself to others.

CURIOSITY

Once, in college, I was asked to write an essay on gifted people throughout history. After researching the backgrounds of Agatha Christie, Michelangelo, Leonardo da Vinci, Mozart, Beethoven, Alexander Graham Bell, Thomas Edison, Benjamin Franklin, and Albert Einstein, I discovered that there was more to them than met the eye. I found that their gifts and accomplishments had little to do with high levels of intelligence. Instead, what these folks had in common was their curiosity and passion about their work, as well as their understanding of how to use this curiosity and passion to their advantage

Curiosity channels and supports out-of-the-box thinking. As an aspiring entrepreneur, you must learn to use curiosity to your advantage by learning how things work and coming up with solutions when things don't work. To arrive at any destination and level of success, finding solutions to problems requires deep curiosity, prompting you to study problems from multiple angles and opening possibilities to improve them.

Being curious also means being present and observing what is necessary for business success. Innovative ideas come from an active and curious mind, and curiosity opens the door to new possibilities. Don't settle for taking ideas at face value. Curious people want to discover the truth for themselves. The late Steve Jobs, former CEO of Apple, once said, "Much of what I stumbled into by following my curiosity and intuition turned out to be priceless later on."[4] Yes, answers to real questions are prompted by a healthy curiosity. However, solving problems is one thing, identifying problems you didn't realize existed is another. This is where curiosity gives you the advantage of growing your business by identifying unexpected yet foreseeable issues and staying ahead of the game.

Curiosity leads to questions, and chasing questions leads to answers and a deeper understanding of the world around you. When I started my jewelry company, I asked many questions. I explored, experimented, and invented new processes for positive outcomes, which brought early and sustained profits and competitive advantage. If you're starting a business and are new to an industry and don't know the established rules, you're more likely to ask questions, experiment, or create new ways of serving your target market. However, be aware that if answers or solutions don't come on the first try, have patience, keep trying, and do not give up. Thomas Edison tried and failed hundreds of times but never gave up, and eventually discovered and invented the first electric light bulb.

CHARACTER

When I hear the word *character*, my mind instantly returns to my childhood as I stood on the shore of Korea, days before we would cross the ocean to a new life. My dad knew the risks, but he trusted his character, his gut, and the drive that lived within him. Since then, I have been convinced that character is an entrepreneur's most essential quality. Success won't come easy, and your character—your honesty, loyalty, integrity, compassion, and resilience—will be tested repeatedly. My own life's greatest disappointments helped strengthen my character. Having survived those mistakes I can now face challenges and confidently make tough decisions. No matter what happens along the way, focus on your character—who you are, not how others see you. You must have integrity and fortitude to do the right thing and keep progressing despite failure. Faced with failure, those without character quit. A person with the strength of character learns from their failures and adapts to the next opportunity. Have you ever asked yourself what is the strength of your character? How important is integrity to you and your venture?

Throughout the years, I've seen brilliant people with great moral values enter the TV retail world, giving their heart and soul to achieve success but compromising their character. Many paid a high price in their personal lives, including divorce and losing relationships with friends and family. In my experience, some of the most successful businesspeople are masters at making compromises, but not in their character. Those who take money for a service or product must stand behind it firmly, confidently, and completely.

Character doesn't require inside connections, expertise, or fancy degrees. It costs nothing, and I find it comforting knowing it can't be bought.

KEY TAKEAWAYS

- Success won't come easy, and your character—honesty, loyalty, integrity, compassion, and resilience—will be tested repeatedly.

- Curiosity leads to out-of-the-box thinking.

- A lack of confidence can lead to self-doubt and fear in individuals, and they may even develop impostor syndrome.

- If you strive to build more confidence, you can better cope with mental stress and understand yourself as a leader.

- You can increase your capabilities over time.

- Confident leaders gain various mental health benefits, such as a positive sense of self-worth, a reduction in stress, and the ability to bounce back after failure.

CHAPTER 6

Building Your Brand and Business

In this ever-changing society, the most powerful and enduring brands are built from the heart. They are real and sustainable. Their foundations are stronger because they are built with the strength of the human spirit, not an ad campaign. The companies that are lasting are those that are authentic.[1]

—HOWARD SCHULTZ

HAVE YOU EVER HEARD OF BRAD'S DRINK? PROBABLY NOT. BUT I guarantee you've tasted the unique concoction—commonly known as Pepsi-Cola. It is also a safe bet that if you ask your parents, grandparents, and even great-grandparents to name popular foods or beverages from their youth, each generation will include Pepsi.

Brad's Drink was named after Caleb Bradham, who, in 1893, invented the delicious and addicting soft drink and brought it to the world.[2] Brad's Drink was eventually renamed Pepsi-Cola and Bradham did pretty well for himself until after World War I, when myriad factors forced him to sell the failing business.

In 1940, the Pepsi-Cola Company made marketing history with its jingle, "Nickel, Nickel," which became an instant classic. More than four decades later, by combining pop music and the current culture, Pepsi changed the trajectory of marketing and advertising once again, featuring Michael Jackson drinking Pepsi in his famous, white-gloved hand. Even though the message was bright and clear, sadly, what happened behind the scenes during the commercial is what sent their name brand into the stratosphere. During the shooting, the performer's hair caught fire. He was severely burned and required numerous painful surgeries. This news caught the world's attention, shining a light on Pepsi products despite the tragedy. Jackson recovered and Pepsi continued its skillful marketing and innovative branding, keeping the Pepsi brand at the forefront and selling soft drinks to millions. But how did they do it?

The answer is Pepsi's strong and simple message, solid identifiable logo, and ability to deliver to every customer. When consumers see Pepsi, they know the brand and the product. However, a logo alone does not make a brand or build a business. It takes a lot more.

Building a brand is essential, and setting your company, large or small, toward growing and building your name and brand will help you maintain and sustain your business for the long term. Amazon's Jeff Bezos once said, "A brand for a company is like a reputation for a person. You earn a reputation by trying to do hard things well."[3] So, does your business have a reputation or even a story to tell? You bet it does. From the moment you opened your doors and the instant you conceived your idea, whether you knew it or not, you've been crafting it. Your marketing and branding began as you carved out a unique niche in your industry, and your marketing will continue with every new product you release. So, do you have a brand that stands out? If not, I want to introduce you to the differences and similarities culminating in a brand's strategy and identity.

There are significant differences between brand strategy and brand identity. It can be as simple as a clever name, term, number, or any other feature that makes your business distinguishable. So, for example, websites are brands, receptionists are brands, and company on-hold messages and even corporate offices can be part of a brand.

For the world to know what a company stands for and consists of, the brand identity messaging must be displayed, spoken, written, explicitly or implicitly, in everything it does. Brands are tools that drive commercial value and help owners, stakeholders, and even investors profit and run their businesses efficiently.

A brand strategy, however, differs vastly from a brand identity. Building a brand requires focus and forces you to think about the one thing you can do better than anyone else. It also requires you to think about your core products and services and how they make new and existing customers feel. How does your product or service benefit your customers? For example, Amazon was built on "customer obsession," and its core product is practicability and expediency. Yes, Amazon sells anything you can imagine, from simple widgets to groceries to luxury goods. However, consumers flock to Amazon because they provide two things: extreme ease of use and modern convenience.

Tesla was built on technology to provide electric cars for a better future for the planet. First, the company identified its key features and benefits: a range of technological innovations, such as gasoline-free, all-electric cars with realistic battery life. Then, with branding messaging, Tesla sold its target audience the idea that by buying one of its vehicles, they could save money while helping save the planet. This was powerful brand messaging at its finest. Tesla went the extra mile by innovating every part of a car owner's experience. It improved how cars are purchased as well as where they can be bought—either online or conveniently at shopping malls where its ideal customers could look at cars during their lunch hour, on their way home from work, and more. Tesla left no stone unturned in building its brand and business simultaneously.

At Rachel & Victoria, our core product is custom-designed, lab-grown diamond engagement rings, necklaces, earrings, bracelets, and anniversary presents for millennials passionate about the future of the planet. After many months of trial and error, we discovered how to build our brand by focusing on our core customers and offering environmentally friendly packaging and recycled precious metals whenever possible.

BRAND STRATEGY

Much like Tesla's and Amazon's, a brand strategy and varying business and marketing strategies are vital to building your business. Although the concept of branding is often confused with simple parts, such as choosing the logo, font, and colors for the website and the packaging of a product, building an enduring brand is much more than that. These are important and necessary elements, but not critical to the long-term growth of your business. Plus, most business owners rarely develop, consider, and document branding strategies since they typically outsource these tasks to freelance graphic designers or media companies. And it is here where many fledgling business owners fail and fall short in following through with a sharply defined brand strategy.

Your brand strategy is your voice and mission. It focuses your business and marketing efforts. Branding aims to let clients understand what your company stands for and how it differs from the competition. In contrast to a detailed marketing strategy, a brand strategy encompasses marketing, product development, sales, and customer service. Besides marketing, the brand refers to the reputation of your organization, product, or service. So, what are the benefits of developing a brand strategy for your business?

One vital element and benefit is defining your business purpose. People don't just care about product features, they care about aligning themselves with a brand that reflects their values and has a clear purpose.

In 2020, Vrity Research found that 55 percent of consumers paid more attention to brand values, and 52 percent said they had bought from a brand for the first time because of its values. Eighty-two percent said they would pick one brand over

another—and pay more—because of their brand values.[4] Therefore, communicating your core identities, such as your purpose,
vision, mission, and values is essential to building a brand strategy.

Another benefit is that a brand strategy helps your company's
image become clear, compelling, and memorable in the minds of
your target audience. The brand strategy must be clear-cut, and
the execution spot-on to create the image you want your audience
to conjure when they think of your company. The goal is to make
your brand enticing and to let customers know without a doubt
what they are getting when buying or using your products or service. Have you ever been on a road trip, seen the Starbucks logo
on an interstate sign, and immediately wanted a cup of coffee?
How do you feel when you see the Starbucks logo? What do you
envision? Does the taste of their coffee make you want to pull off
the highway to get one? This is the power of branding at its best,
and this is what you need to strive for.

In addition to benefiting your customers, branding conveys
the actions, stances, and words that reflect your company's values.
Finally, brand strategy is about telling your brand's story to your
customers so they understand why your company exists.

When I started Rachel & Victoria, I was in the dark about
my brand strategy. But through trial and error I determined my
market demographic for my products. My background, upbring-
ing, and the adversity I faced in bringing my jewelry to the world
became part of my brand identity. Strategic brand storytelling
highlights the reasons behind your company's existence, the journey that led you to where you are today, and the values and principles you hold dear, connecting you and your customers at a deeper
level. It keeps your customers loyal to your brand since they feel
good about supporting it. The strategy should also be aligned with
your short-, mid-, and long-term goals, so you and your team can
make well-informed decisions as your business grows.

BUSINESS STRATEGY

Since we discussed *brand strategy*, we must now look at *business strategy* and the significant difference between the two. A business strategy allows you to enhance and reach your aspiration for your company by focusing on your business's vision, mission, goals, and how you plan to achieve them. Business strategies, unlike branding strategy, are the engines that drive, focusing more on the inside work and how your business will succeed in the market, while brand strategies focus more on how clients perceive your message. A business strategy examines your business's strengths, weaknesses, opportunities, and competition. Specifically, a business strategy looks at market trends, differentiation, technology, partnerships, and even business models to determine how your company can perform better. However, your business strategy doesn't focus on promoting your products or services because that's where marketing strategy comes into play.

MARKETING STRATEGY

A marketing strategy is shaped by a company's brand and business strategies. So, consider how to market your business and use social networks to create a marketing strategy. Using your brand and business strategies, you can create a marketing strategy that encourages buyers and reinforces the essence of your brand. To create an effective marketing strategy, you must identify your clients, your position in the market, your strengths, and your weaknesses.

It is best to determine how to use your brand and business strategy to promote your products and services. Brand, business, and marketing strategies must be integrated successfully to ensure your company's success. Having mastered each branch individually, you can combine them for more sales, followers, and clients.

But what is marketing? The answer may sound simple but will probably vary from person to person. As a student, I was taught that marketing is a set of processes for communicating with and delivering value to prospective customers. Traditionally, marketing avenues such as television, radio, mail, and word-of-mouth were used. In addition to traditional marketing, digital marketing includes email, social media, affiliate marketing, and content marketing. Marketing aims to identify the ideal customer for your product or service and keep attracting them.

As a discipline, marketing involves all company activities that attract customers and maintain relationships with them. The work also includes networking with past or potential clients, including writing thank-you emails, attending personal and professional events, and even simple things such as returning phone calls promptly or meeting clients and customers for a cup of coffee. In its simplest form, marketing aims to match a company's products and services with customers who want them, and when successfully done, almost guarantees profitability.

While in college, I was taught a marketing tool, which I later implemented to get my business off the ground, called the four Ps, also known as a marketing mix. The four core areas are: price, promotion, place, and products.

Price

Your product or service must be competitively priced, offering value. However, you do not need to be the lowest-priced option in the marketplace. For example, you can be the highest-priced competitor in the luxury goods sector and still enjoy a significant market share.

Promotion

There are endless ways to promote your products, such as advertising, email newsletters, contests, free publicity, and more. However, do not confuse promotion with sales. In today's marketplace, consumers require you to reach out to them via email, ad campaigns, social media posts, etc. many times before they make a purchase.

Therefore, trying to close a sale before your ideal customers are ready and eager to purchase is not a sustainable strategy.

Place

You must offer your clients many different ways to make a purchase. Even if your business is located in an ideal mall location, you must provide more ways for your customers to make their purchases, such as a website, affiliate websites, and/or creating multiple special events at various locations so your customers can "experience" your products or service.

Products

When it comes to the success and longevity of your business, everything starts with your product. First, ensure your product offers a competitive edge over all others on the market. Being the lowest-priced vendor is usually not a great competitive edge because some vendor always goes out of business and dumps similar goods for ridiculous prices. Ensure you are constantly in touch with your product development and how your customers experience your products. All of my jewelry products have evolved with technology to help source better quality gemstones, better equipment to manufacture, and fresh styles to keep up with changing tastes. Instead of focusing on one message, effective marketing encompasses a wide range of topics. And by keeping the four Ps in mind, marketing professionals focus on what matters and reach a wider audience. Organizations like yours can make strategic decisions based on an ideal marketing mix when launching new products or revising existing ones. Even with these core areas in place, marketing is much more nuanced and less vague. Also, there is a lot of noise in the promotional arena because of multiple messages, price-sensitive consumers, complex products, and a wide range of channels used to reach a company's intended audience.

THE BIG PICTURE

Your goal is to grasp the tried-and-true knowledge of strategic marketing and to have long-term success in marketing. No matter how crowded, convoluted, or complicated, every marketer must address the brand itself and the message being put forth. And with your marketing focusing and investing in campaigns, channels, and tactics, it's essential to maintain flexibility during this process and use marketing data to support your position. Trust the process, but always remember that marketing is a progression. It must be done in increments, determining what works and what doesn't. If your marketing strategy is successful, your ideal customers will be exposed to your brand and feel a connection that drives intended purchase behavior. And if you deliver on your brand's marketing promise, customers will remain loyal and give you the feedback you need to maintain their dedication and attract new audiences.

THE DIFFERENCE IN BRAND BUILDING AND BUILDING A BUSINESS

Many marketing and business gurus teach that building a business is not complicated. They promote the idea that starting a business is as simple as figuring out what you want to offer, how you'll supply it, and then finding the people who want what you're offering. While that is all accurate in the real sense of building a business, there is a lot more to the process. For example, a brand is something different, another organism in and of itself. It's the difference between Coca-Cola, Starbucks, Apple, and the unbranded fizzy drinks, copycat coffee brands, and knockoff imitations scattered across the marketplace. In short, a business finds new customers, while brands focus on the people they already have in their circle to create value.

So, your brand and business are two essential yet different business concepts that seem similar but should be treated separately. Building a brand defines your business, while your business strategy focuses on using your brand to make profits. You cannot build a business without first defining your brand. So, the two concepts should work together to meet your goals.

Looking at this from a broad view, your brand is the face of your business, but your "business" is the internal mechanism and processes that lead to profits and growth. Compared to branding, which is the art of making people care about your business and connecting with your audience, building a business is about products and services, assigning tangible goals for profits and positive outcomes. Branding falls back on the customer's experience, how you want them to feel about your business, and your agency's culture and values. The business is about how the customer experience will convert to profits for your company. Theoretically, any entity that generates income—has more money coming in than going out—is a business. However, by running and growing a business, you consistently generate substantially more revenue than it costs to run your business by taking the proper steps in building your brand.

Unfortunately, many fledgling entrepreneurs mistake their brand-building with mirrored business success. This isn't exactly how it works—there is more. Idowu Koyenikan, in his book *Wealth for All: Living a Life of Success at the Edge of Your Ability*, writes, "You have to work on the business first before it works for you."[5] To see this in action, one must examine the world's most iconic brands and how they have mastered their branding message and built their business to generate billions in sales. Super successful brands like Dom Perignon, Channel, Amazon, Target, McDonald's, Apple, Costco, Trader Joe's, and Tesla consistently attract consumers with relatively less effort than their competitors.

These brands enjoy immense loyalty from their existing customers and easily attract new customers. At first glance, you may wonder what the difference is. Many beginner entrepreneurs understand that building a brand is something they want and need to do in their journey, but they don't make a conscious effort toward building their brand to generate a healthy business and bottom line—until it's too late.

A BUSINESS IS FOCUSED ON SALES—A BRAND IS FOCUSED ON COMMUNITY

Building a brand should aim to grow a community, with the broader goal of generating income for your business. A strong community ensures sales, so branding and business are important. Brands are not grown by the number of products they sell or leads they generate—they are developed by engagement, reach, and recognition. In contrast to building a business, building a brand usually involves focusing on what you want your brand to embody. As a business, you can solve the needs within the community you create, and as a brand, you can reach more people whose needs your business can help or solve. Even though these concepts can work independently, the most successful companies build their brand alongside their business.

NUTS AND BOLTS OF BUILDING AND SCALING A BUSINESS

As your business grows, you will often discover new ways to maintain efficiency and profitability, which involves strategic scaling for longevity. Scaling a business helps you as an entrepreneurial leader guide your team by implementing and testing new processes or procedures to reduce risk, preparing your organization for short- and long-term growth.

Business scaling is the process of ensuring a business grows without sacrificing quality or increasing costs. Increasing sales volumes while steadily reducing costs is the hallmark of a successfully scaled business. Businesses can support long-term growth and profitability by effectively planning and preparing systems, staff, and processes. In addition, by scaling, a growing company can ensure cost-effective production and an effective workforce. The key to scaling a business is adapting to a new way of doing business, not just increasing sales or inventory turnover.

When scaling, you must consider your product offering, marketing, funding sources, internal processes, staffing, business premises, and infrastructure. Finally, explore how your company can increase its operational capacity to handle more sales or work without disrupting current operations. An organized, sustainable, adaptable, and effective plan can help you reach your goals.

Every globally successful company began small but was actively scaled after its launch. Certain factors undoubtedly played a vital role in how those organizations grew and became successful, including products or services that solved a customer problem, perceived value of that product or service, timely delivery of that product, worldwide reach, high gross margin, and the fact that no friction existed between the elements of the business model that would prevent scaling.

Growing a business is challenging, and learning from failures can sometimes be time-consuming, expensive, and frustrating. Yet one critical challenge must be met by securing suitable, agreeable, and affordable financial support as you scale your business. Business scaling before experiencing sales growth can be expensive. Set realistic and clear targets for all business areas as you scale. Consider everything, such as sales growth, cost management, staff recruitment and training, and how scaling and growth might affect your business in the long term. A business plan for growth that outlines clear metrics for success in all departments will help you and every team member understand their role in the company's growth and future. When creating goals, consider combining short- and long-term objectives to help track progress at every turn. Significant, but sustainable, growth is often better for a business than uncontrolled growth. Setting realistic goals will help you avoid financial ruin.

KEY TAKEAWAYS

- Building a brand helps you grow your business faster because it cultivates brand loyalty and allows you to generate new customers more quickly.

- Know the difference between building a business and building a brand. When you generate more revenue than costs, you have a business. However, building a brand with brand loyalty and recognition will help you attract partners and investors and ultimately provide you with a viable exit strategy for selling your business, if you wish to, at a premium.

- The importance of providing a quality and consistent product cannot be overstated.

- Competitive pricing does not mean the lowest price on the market. Instead, your pricing must deliver the most value for the product category.

- Set realistic and clear targets for all business areas as you scale.

- A brand identity can be as simple as a clever name, term, number, or any other company feature that distinguishes it from others.

- For the world to know what a company stands for and comprises, the brand identity messaging must be displayed, spoken, written (explicitly or implicitly) in everything it does.

- Brands are tools that drive commercial value and help owners, stakeholders, even investors earn profit and run their businesses efficiently.

- A brand strategy differs vastly from a brand identity in the business world.

- Building a brand requires extreme focus and forces you to think about the one thing you can do better than anyone else.

- Building a business and brand requires you to think about your core products and how those products or services make new and existing customers feel.

CHAPTER 7

Selling Your Products on TV

Everyone lives by selling something.[1]

—ROBERT LOUIS STEVENSON

LET ME TAKE YOU ON A TOUR OF AMERICAN SHOPPING CHANNEL history. As the first major business to combine two popular American pastimes, shopping and watching television, the Home Shopping Network (HSN) became a success. Once this phenomenon took America by storm, many imitators emerged onto the TV retailing landscape. Yet HSN stood firm as it expanded from its small beginnings on a Florida radio station to a multibillion-dollar corporation with over five million customers.

Launched in St. Petersburg, Florida, HSN featured a revolutionary concept of having attractive, perky hosts advertise items live on the air for viewers who could then order their products over the phone. HSN began by selling to older, middle-class, and working-class American consumers. It was a winning combination, as the idea of shopping without leaving home had great appeal to the viewing public. In addition, the company soon discovered it could easily sell the most popular products, including costume jewelry, cooking pots and utensils, house-cleaning equipment, and celebrity clothing and cosmetic lines. As a result, HSN's growth skyrocketed, and by 1985 it was carried on major cable networks and had over seventy-five thousand regular subscribers.

At the same time, cable TV was beginning to expand into the American television market, opening a vast broadcast arena that had never existed before. Almost anyone with broadcast experience could start their own channel, and cable channels quickly became ubiquitous. Unfortunately, two things happened: First, several young, fledgling channels and networks that relied on advertising revenue started losing money after attracting less-than-stellar ratings. Next, the religious channels realized their fundraising efforts in the wee hours and late evenings were failing miserably.

In all this, space for cheap broadcasting was created as enterprising businesspeople swallowed up the carcasses of the dying cable industry like vultures, purchasing blocks of time in the late-night, off-peak broadcasting hours. They started repurposing inexpensively produced sixty-minute commercials as entertainment programs. And from this, it didn't take long for infomercial superstars to emerge from a cast of unknowns, all pitching mongers who found fame and fortune. With her exercise tapes, Jane Fonda created lightning in a bottle, boosting the video and infomercial businesses to heights never imagined. Those of a certain age will never forget the powerful messaging of the late Billy Mays and his bombastic pitch of OxiClean, leading the product to sell millions.

However, as always with new, thriving industries, imitators and innovators tried to cash in immediately after their initial infomercial success, and as usual, most of them failed. Likewise, the infomercial industry was overwhelmed with wannabes, resulting in production rates skyrocketing and broadcast time becoming increasingly expensive. As a result, the infomercial industry went from nothing to enviable annual revenues almost overnight, despite knockoffs and failures. With that success, the infomercial industry became a precursor to HSN and QVC, which essentially air mini infomercials twenty-four hours a day with spokespeople hyperfocused on sales. Fortunately, we no longer have to listen to loud-mouthed hucksters and midnight men hawk the latest "it slices" and "it dices" products. Instead, TV retailing is a viable and profit-generating avenue that is professional and, if done correctly, highly profitable. Even though many of the infomercial superstars' taglines still bring back memories of the good old days, running and creating costly infomercials differs vastly from selling your products on TV networks such as HSN, QVC, and ShopHQ. Unfortunately, traditional TV advertising has a high cost. Even in smaller local markets, a thirty-second ad can cost thousands. Compared to paid advertising and infomercials, TV retailing and selling is another world, and no other marketing strategy exposes your brand to one hundred million people at once. And no matter what industry you're in, especially if you're selling physical products, at the onset of your business, you're probably busy focusing most of your efforts on production, marketing, and distribution. But nowhere in the marketing field is your brand and product exposed to tens of millions of potential consumers other than on TV. So if you want to expand on a large scale, TV retailing with large networks is one of the most effective ways to expand and grow your business.

The business world is constantly evolving, and companies are trying to reach a larger audience with new and creative strategies, but TV retailing and shopping continues to flourish and remain effective. However, many new businesses and entrepreneurs overlook the benefits of placing their products on shopping networks such as HSN, QVC, and ShopHQ. Many believe getting on TV is impossible and that selling to millions isn't feasible. But today, companies like yours face two of the biggest challenges when launching a product: adequate customer reach and effective product representation. TV meets those needs and more. Companies like yours can use these networks to tell your story and make your product relatable to consumers while reaching a significantly larger audience. The QVC network reaches three hundred million homes worldwide through broadcast programming. It is available in the US, UK, Germany, Japan, Italy, France, and China. Domestically, HSN reaches ninety-five million homes and broadcasts twenty-four hours a day, seven days a week. Unlike your average infomercial, these networks offer exclusive deals and competitive pricing. In addition, they closely monitor the market to ensure customers get the best live and real-time deals possible.

As consumers, most of us seek ways to do things faster and easier everywhere in the marketplace. And now, with mobile devices, millions can shop anywhere, anytime. Perhaps you've discovered a solution or invention that solves a problem for millions of people. If so, good for you, and one of the greatest ways of showing its potential is on TV where consumers can see products in action and understand how they will solve their problems, which is impossible in other retail settings.

Another aspect that makes TV retail so attractive for your business, aside from saving time and energy, is that the hosts may play a key role in encouraging viewers to make informed buying decisions quickly. Over time, some viewers develop a pseudo-relationship with shopping show hosts, who employ various conversational tactics to encourage viewer interaction. As a result, the TV seller (you), using your story and conversation, can address the problem, show its potential, and provide the solution, repeating the message and process, driving positive results, and leading to significant sales.

Most TV networks are publicly owned and regulated, and their platforms allow a salesperson to express themselves creatively while following all laws and regulations. They showcase products in various formats, including live demonstrations, animation, still images, stories, props, customer testimonials, and videos. Many of these stories are repeated throughout the airing to ensure the messaging resonates with the audience, leading to sales. And once you have the tools in place, you can strengthen your product's brand positioning by using TV broadcasts as an integral part of your marketing strategy, reaching a wider audience, and ensuring the message you built your product around grabs your intended customers and beyond.

ADVANTAGES OF TV RETAILING

Besides massive exposure and increased sales revenues, you may wonder about the other advantages of selling on these different TV networks for your business. There are numerous advantages to selling your products on TV networks, especially during the active growth stage of your business. Consider the fact that most notable TV networks, such as QVC, HSN, and ShopHQ, have an unparalleled market share, reaching millions of consumers with cable TV channels. I've worked with many TV retailers worldwide and made good profit margins for over twenty-five years through trial and error of learning to understand my target audience. To do this with my jewelry, I had to combat the disadvantages while reaping the benefits and awards offered by the TV retailing world. While I've sold millions of jewelry pieces in my thirty-five-year career, those numbers were only possible through television selling, perfecting my pitch, and driving home the power of compelling storytelling. There are many advantages to pitching your product to a shopping channel besides the obvious fame and fortune. Shopping channels offer countless opportunities and advantages such as:

- Access to millions of consumers instantly
- Large-scale purchase orders
- Instant feedback
- The opportunity to showcase your best salesperson
- An endorsement of your trustworthiness and credibility
- Exposure to new audiences

77

- Contenting and product testing
- Performance optimization

Access to Millions of Consumers Instantly

Most TV retailers today provide instant exposure to millions of consumers nationwide that entrepreneurs would otherwise not have access to. That sort of exposure can skyrocket your business. It stands to reason that smaller brands want to grow, and big brands want to stay big. A recent Nielsen report says Americans still watch four and a half hours of television per day, despite increasingly interacting with brands through digital and social media.[2] When your products are featured on a shopping channel, they get millions of impressions across one hundred million households in the US, and you need not pay for airtime. Shopping channels also leverage digital and social channels, creating a shop-anytime experience.

Large-Scale Purchase Orders

One of the benefits of doing business with TV networks is that since they order in large volumes, an entrepreneur can take advantage of the economies of scale and get much better pricing on raw materials or finished goods. It's even possible to negotiate lower shipping costs on all goods sold by your company because you will get favorable pricing and terms from your entire supply chain. In addition, TV retailers buy extraordinarily massive quantities of each item. In 1998, when I first sold my products to HSN, they routinely ordered ten to thirty thousand units of jewelry every month, compared to my top-tier department stores, which would order one to two thousand pieces *per year* of similarly priced items.

Instant Feedback

Most TV retailers track their sales by item, color, or size while you are live on air. If they bought 3,000 units of an item that retails for $100 and gave you ten minutes to sell them, but you end up selling 2,500 units in the first five minutes, averaging 500 units per minute, they would immediately be looking for some other item to sell for four minutes. Of course, your audience would have no way of knowing that this item was scheduled for a ten-minute presentation, but they might feel the excitement surrounding this product as some sizes and colors sell out. This is instant feedback. In this scenario, you're getting an excellent response.

Furthermore, while you're live on air, you can see which colors and sizes are most and least popular. In a regular department store setting, this type of feedback takes weeks, sometimes an entire season. Most TV retailers welcome testimonials, questions, and feedback from their viewing audience. These testimonial calls validate the quality and value of your product, how it is being used, what your customers like most about your product, and their firsthand experience with it. I've even received design ideas from some testimonial calls. The most positive aspect is that these testimonials might persuade hesitant customers to make a purchase during your presentation. For example, when I show my jewelry for several hours on the same day, within a few minutes I get instant feedback on the twelve to sixteen styles I'm presenting and discover which were the top sellers. With the feedback I receive from actual sales data and testimonial calls, I can tweak my upcoming shows on the same day with the help of my producer, buyer, and planner. And during the presentation, the customer call-ins affirming their purchase further support the presentation, which leads to hitting my numbers and generating substantial sales. Plus, instant feedback is essential in designing, developing, and keeping products that sell well for other future offerings.

The Opportunity to Showcase Your Best Salesperson

Selling on TV allows you to have your best salesperson present your products to millions of potential customers, showcasing everything through a perfectly crafted brand story, features, and benefits. For most entrepreneurs, the opportunity to put their best salesperson and product directly in front of millions of people is a game changer. Sometimes the best salesperson for your brand is you. After all, you know your products better than anyone. Being the face of your product and brand opens enormous possibilities for building and growing your brand with you as a TV personality.

An Endorsement of Your Trustworthiness and Credibility
Shopping channels are notoriously selective about what products they sell, and for a good reason. They're trying to keep their customers happy. TV shopping channels are also highly regulated and subject to the laws of the state in which they operate. In addition, federal agencies such as the Federal Trade Commission (FTC) regulate them. I've done business with major department stores and TV networks, and I promise you that the quality control standards were much higher at TV shopping networks than at major brick-and-mortar store chains. TV shopping networks cannot risk having an on-air personality who doesn't stick to facts or someone who does not resonate with their viewing audience. Presenting your product on a major TV shopping network is an explicit endorsement of your trustworthiness and credibility, telling viewers and customers that your product is unique, excellent, and worth checking out. Besides expediting approval from customers, other retailers, and e-tailers, your on-air presence means you survived the approval process and have what it takes to be on the air. As a result, retailers like you can use TV exposure to sell your goods and strengthen your brand.

Exposure to New Audiences
Shopping on TV is a favorite pastime for many people, and TV shopping networks often enjoy a high rate of repeat purchases. Victoria Wieck Jewelry, my brand, has an exceptionally high brand loyalty index, with over 80 percent of customers making repeat purchases. The lure of TV shopping is strong. It's a visual shopping venue where products are described and demonstrated

on your TV screen. Unfortunately, it's no secret that most department stores, big-box retailers, and other stores generally do not offer sales personnel with experience or knowledge of their products. It's been my experience that on the rare occasion I've ventured into the shopping mall, I've had to brave the notorious Los Angeles traffic, then circle the parking lot endlessly for parking only to find that the department store was out of stock on the item I was looking for. In addition, I often can't find a salesperson who could find out if I could order it. Many big-box stores sell their products without ever demonstrating them. This is not the case with TV retailing, as products are thoroughly presented and explained right in your living room and come with an unconditional thirty-day, money-back guarantee. The return policy at many big-box stores, by contrast, are less than thirty days and come with a whole list of conditions.

You might think that TV shopping networks are most popular in rural America, where millions of people live in areas without access to large retail stores and malls. While TV shopping offers a real solution to rural America with only a few shopping centers, the reality is that most TV shopping networks perform best in states with abundant shopping choices. For example, the best market for my products, for both Victoria Wieck Jewelry and Rachel & Victoria, is California, followed by New York, Florida, and Texas, in that order. The whole experience of TV shopping is about building an emotional connection with millions of potential customers. I believe that when millions of people fall in love with you and your products, you are well on your way to building a fantastic brand. And for you, as an innovative entrepreneur, reaching new audiences can take your business from small to a household name.

Content and Product Testing

Product testing is essential for both startups as well as for mega brands. If you look closely, even well-established brands still conduct focus groups and product testing before launching new products. In fact, the bigger the brand name, the more money they spend on product testing because mega brands cannot afford negative publicity arising from a product that doesn't work. TV retailers understand and conduct product and content testing better than any other type of business. They can offer variations of the concept in real-time due to their ability to obtain instant feedback from real customers. Also, they can perfect their messaging to their customers in a matter of minutes. During my live TV shows, my producer often relays real-time feedback that I can use to perfect my pitch. For instance, during one live show, I mentioned I like to design jewelry that offers versatility so my customers can wear it to work, semiformal occasions, or even to their children's soccer game, etc. A couple of minutes later, my producer relayed to me in my earpiece, "Vic, when you mentioned your kid's soccer, the call volume shot straight up, and we're almost out of time, so we are moving on to the next item now." So what my producer told me is that my audience likes the inspiration behind my entire semicasual, highly versatile styling. From then on, my messaging evolved around well-crafted jewelry you can proudly wear anywhere without spending a fortune. The advantage of TV retailing is controlling the content and tracking the response to your messages and concepts. Then, using this new, fun media to fine tune your compelling messaging, you can engage more with your viewers, scoring a huge win that can be rolled out across other distribution channels.

Performance Optimization

Shopping channels have precise metrics. These analytics enable innovative brands to optimize every aspect of their business, from productivity to continuity. With this knowledge, getting started can be less intimidating as you approach the TV shopping business. Live, in front of the camera, TV shopping channel talents see three tracks: what's playing in real-time, the next shot, and how many people are trying to buy. The monitors show how long a product has been on the air, how many people have it in their digital shopping carts, how many people speak to live operators, and how many people are waiting on hold. This is all in real-time and is prepared when you present your product. This inside look is the key to understanding what to expect on set during your presentation.

One of the many benefits of starting a business in today's marketplace is that there are numerous ways to start and grow your business. In my thirty-five-year career as an entrepreneur, I've tried various methods of growing my business without spending a fortune on advertising. Getting your products on TV is one of the best ways to get much-needed product exposure and generate large-scale sales revenues. But how do you get your products on TV, and does it cost a lot of money? The answer is simple. It doesn't have to. Let's explore the advantages and some not-so-helpful methods to get your products on TV.

Advantages of TV Advertising

Traditional TV advertising offers significant audience reach. During prime time, television advertising has the potential to reach a massive audience, providing visibility for your company and brand. TV commercials are often seen and remembered more than other forms of advertising, such as the famous Super Bowl commercials. Furthermore, they are more likely to be seen by a wider audience than other forms of advertising. TV advertising propels your company and brand through audience recognition, helping you establish a powerful presence in the market.

TV advertising also has the advantage of great flexibility in terms of content, timing, and budget. In my experience, the best efforts of TV provide emotional impact and connection with viewers, which can lead to long-term brand loyalty.

However, the downside to TV advertising is that there is always a significant outlay of advertising dollars to produce a commercial or infomercial. Depending on the type of media market, a thirty-second ad can cost tens of thousands of dollars, making straight TV advertising an option but, unfortunately, out of reach for most small business owners. However, infomercials cost less money than traditional TV advertising commercials. Infomercial producers buy large blocks of time during off-peak hours to get a considerable enough discount. And producing a two-minute or thirty-minute show surrounding a specific product is a good thing, but running in the wee hours of the night, in most cases, does not produce the results you seek compared to the cost.

TV advertising is expensive, especially for small businesses with limited budgets. And for the money, the return on investment is small because some networks and TV stations have limited reach to the geographical area in which the commercial airs. Plus, with the technology and ability to bypass commercials, viewers have short attention spans with TV commercials. So, it's essential to ensure your message is concise and memorable. Along with these disadvantages, another negative aspect of TV advertising is that it's difficult to measure a TV ad's effectiveness since there is no way to accurately track how many people actually saw it.

DISADVANTAGES OF TV RETAILING

I would be remiss if I didn't point out some of the disadvantages of TV retailing. The main disadvantage of selling on TV shopping networks is the lack of accurate information. Every industry offers a unique way of doing business that works for them. For example, TV shopping networks judge every product on a dollar per minute, while major department stores judge their product offerings on a dollar per square foot. Of course, there are many other conditions for doing business with vendors, but accurate information regarding TV networks is tough to come by. The TV shopping industry is a highly competitive marketplace, and it can be difficult for small businesses to stand out from the competition. Here are some additional disadvantages to TV retailing:

* Competitive to enter
* High stakes and risk
* Challenging business terms

Competitive to Enter

The TV retail industry is highly competitive and difficult to break into. Every entrepreneur dreams of having their products shown, bought, and loved by many, but breaking into television is not for the faint of heart. It requires drive, perseverance, and thick skin, but the effort is worth it. In addition, TV airtime is their most prized asset, and they guard it at all costs. Unlike traditional department or specialty stores, TV retailers generate all their sales through live TV shows, with some Internet sales. Since there are only twenty-four hours a day for their live programming, they tend to grant airtime to products (and personalities) that they believe will be the most productive. In other words, before you can get any airtime, you must convince them that you will be more successful than the thousands of others vying for slots, which is not easy. Therefore, navigating the complex world of TV retailing may take years.

High Stakes and Risk

High stakes lead to considerable risk. TV retailers judge their vendor partners on average dollars per minute. A dollar-per-minute criterion is also applied to most infomercial retailers. Traditional TV retailers, about thirty who offer 24/7 TV retailing, exist worldwide, with productivity requirements ranging from a few hundred dollars per minute to several thousand. This means that you must understand what each TV shopping network requires from its vendors before you sign any contracts. I've had many occasions where a good friend or colleague told me how excited they were because they finally got on a major TV shopping network. The products flew out the door, but the network informed them that they didn't meet their dollars-per-minute (DPM) requirements. For a small business owner, selling three hundred units of dresses in fifteen minutes sounds like a lot, especially at $60 a dress. But in the TV shopping world, this was nothing short of a disaster for an extensive network. I recommend doing some research about the particular network you want to approach before you send your first solicitation email.

Challenging Business Terms

TV retailers know that nearly every entrepreneur dreams of having their products sold on their network. They know they are in the driver's seat and can demand stringent terms of doing business. This can make TV retailers challenging to deal with. Generally speaking, the bigger the network, the less advantageous its terms will be for you. For example, they may require a portion of the unsold goods be returned to you for full credit if your products do not meet their DPM requirements. If a TV retailer orders ten thousand bottles of shampoo, and the product doesn't meet the DPM threshold, their terms may allow them to return some or all of the unsold goods. A lot of the terms depend on the strength of your brand. For some more established brands, the TV retailer may differentiate between a brand that misses its goal by 70 percent as opposed to a brand that misses its sales goal by 5 percent. In the worst-case scenario, if they purchase ten thousand bottles of shampoo at $5 per bottle but only sell four thousand units, they can return up to the six thousand unsold units, leaving you holding the bag and the leftover inventory. The problem with this scenario is that it's difficult for most small business owners to unload six thousand units within a reasonable amount of time and generate a profit. Ensure you understand the terms and prepare to adhere to them, allowing yourself a fail-safe plan if things do not go as expected.

GETTING STARTED ON TV

Once your product is ready to roll out, you join the many inventors and entrepreneurs with products or gadgets to sell and dream of getting on QVC, HSN, ShopHQ, or other TV shopping channels worldwide. Most of these networks are seen in 250 million homes worldwide. No other retail market allows you to simultaneously expose your brand to that many homes. It isn't easy. It will take perseverance, tenacity, and the will to succeed. There will be planning, preparation, and a ton of market research to peel back the many layers of the complex onion of TV retailing.

I do not want to generalize, but with very few exceptions, the best way to sell on TV is to embrace the three Ps:

• Product
• Personality
• Price

Product

Your product needs to be unique and genuinely add value to the life of your customers. A successful, amazing product appeals to a wide range of customers and stands out from its competitors. The product should differentiate itself from other products on the market and provide users with a unique experience. A successful product should have a clear purpose and value proposition that resonates with customers and meets their needs.

There are several significant factors to consider when defining a successful, unique product. First, a quality product starts with a well-engineered design and high-quality materials. An attractive and exciting design is another essential characteristic of a successful, unique product. And always remember that the product should clearly show how it can help customers meet their goals and expectations. Finally, give your product or service a unique selling point that distinguishes it from other products in the same category by highlighting its personal benefits.

Personality

It's no secret that an outstanding personality, who can explain and demonstrate your product and inspire the audience, can humanize and personalize a product. Most TV products are sold by relatable, trustworthy personalities who can speak about the product with authority. Most TV shopping networks I've worked with look for experts who can present products with authority in a manner that inspires their audience to try their channel. Being a successful TV salesperson isn't easy because many factors, such as authenticity, honesty, and relatability, are hard to measure. It all comes down to personality. While it may seem obvious that an upbeat, vibrant personality will help you sell your product and succeed, there is more to personality and the use of it to move products or market your services. There are many personality traits that TV shopping audiences value, such as expertise in the product category, relatability, trustworthiness, and authenticity. However, the personality trait that TV audiences respond to most is the ability to share your vulnerability. Many entrepreneurs who finally get to showcase their products on TV waste this incredible opportunity by appearing too pushy, unrelatable, or not credible. I've appeared on multiple TV shopping networks, and I've seen my share of movie stars and famous athletes, whom I've outperformed. As of this writing, I've been on live TV shopping networks for over twenty-five years continuously, that makes me one of the longest-running TV shopping personalities in the US, if not the world. I've seen that many famous people who built their fame and fortune in other industries, such as sports, music, and entertainment, assume that their fans would buy cookware or pajamas just because it has their name on it. That strategy rarely works because consumers understand that being an elite athlete may make you an expert in tennis shoes or fitness gear but not necessarily in cookware or jewelry. The few celebrities who could turn their fame into a merchandising success were those who aligned their products to their expertise and worked tirelessly to gain the trust and loyalty of their viewers by being authentic and relatable when presenting their products on TV shopping networks.

All entrepreneurs and businesses are more than their products. A superior product is rarely enough to convince someone to buy it. This makes selling and entrepreneurship challenging, as the importance of having a compelling on-air personality cannot be stressed enough. As most companies' brands and marketing strive to add personality to the business, having the right spokesperson makes all the difference. Your attitude will shape the customers' views and feelings about the product, company, and brand based on your personality. How customers view and interact with you on TV often determines how they feel about the company and anything you sell, do, or make. If you want clients to make a positive, confident choice, your personality must convey that confidence.

Speaking from personal experience, there is no such thing as overnight success in the TV shopping world. My journey from a shy, introverted person to becoming one of the most influential TV personalities in the TV shopping world was full of constant testing, learning, and evolving. On August 11, 1989, I had my first TV shopping hour. I was so frightened of being on live TV, and I remember throwing up in the hotel room all day and feeling like I was about to pass out. I kept telling myself that whatever is said on live TV in front of millions of people can't ever be unsaid. The idea that I needed to keep talking for two solid hours was terrifying. When the time came, I did not know which of the five cameras I should speak to, and it was hard to figure out what I was supposed to say. It took me only a few minutes to figure out that I just needed to be my authentic self, be as brutally honest as possible with the audience, and present my designs, describing their features, benefits, and the inspiration behind them. In hindsight, my authenticity and vulnerability were precisely the qualities the customers responded to. The viewers saw I was nervous and new to the TV shopping world. However, they also knew that the stories I shared about my inspirations behind each design were authentic, and they found my stories interesting and relatable. To this day, I'm still hearing from customers who watched my first TV appearance and have been cheering for me ever since.

In my opinion, a good TV spokesperson must have the drive to succeed without being pushy. Motivated and ambitious, they must be able to withstand the intensity that TV brings. Unfortunately, many newcomers mistakenly talk about themselves and their products when marketing to customers. Prospective customers aren't interested in you—they're interested in how your product will benefit them and improve their lives.

So, having a charismatic personality is always a plus. Interacting naturally and being open, honest, and friendly with others helps your sales. There is something almost mystical about charisma, magnetism, and allure—customers flock to it when it's delivered correctly. Some people naturally have charm and charisma, but it can't be learned by those who don't. You are either charming or not. But don't worry; you can conceal a lack of charisma if you learn to be likable. So how do you do that? The answer is target audience research. Finding what drives your target audience's sense of purpose and what keeps them up at night is vital to achieving this.

Knowing your audience and determining who wants to buy your product is essential. Author Pooka Agnihotri, in her book *17 Reasons Why Businesses Fail: Unscrew Yourself from Business Failures*, writes, "Knowing your audience well as a part of the market research will pay off with improved customer loyalty and relationship building."[3] Every product has a customer. A key aspect of television retailing is knowing who that customer is and the problem you are solving for them. At any juncture, if you are unsure of who your customers are, conduct thorough market research to learn this information. I can't stress this point enough. Like everything else in life, you must conduct research before you can craft the best story and pitch to approach any TV retailer and buying team.

I've spent countless days with buyers of TV networks, and the common feedback I've received is that they wished potential vendors performed thorough market research for their product category. Many have stressed they wished vendors focused on market trends and research on their intended audience, crafting their product and pitching with them in focus. TV retailers are approached hundreds, even thousands, of times each week by potential vendors via email, phone calls, and unsolicited samples. These buyers must attend endless internal and external meetings, working long hours to meet their numbers. Since their TV store is open 24/7, crises and opportunities arise at a moment's notice, and they do not want to educate any potential vendor on the "basics of TV selling." They do not have the time. That is your job. I've spent countless hours with buyers from multiple TV retailers. I can tell you definitively that if you do your homework and incorporate the info you've gathered in your opening pitch to any TV buyer, you will significantly increase your chances of getting an appointment. This will take some research, but it will be worthwhile.

With charisma and an upbeat personality, credible personalities, such as the founder or inventor of your product or celebrities who regularly use it, can tell compelling stories about your product, significantly increasing sales dollars per minute. Using the strength of your personality or the characterization of a celebrity to pitch your product is essential for TV retail success.

Price

Pricing your product becomes relevant only if it is unique and you can present it on TV with credibility. While it's true that people care about the price they pay, they want to get the right product that helps them solve a problem from someone they know and trust. On average, TV reaches nearly 90 percent of adults, and TV retailing influences more consumer buying decisions than any other retail medium. Even the smallest businesses can access the power of TV selling thanks to the variety of shopping channels and services available.

STEPS AND PRINCIPLES FOR TELEVISION

Many people ask me how a product can be successfully marketed on a TV shopping channel. The first step is to honestly self-assess your product or service. Are you ready to pitch? Is your product or service well-developed and ready for prime time? Examine your business and prepare earnestly to pitch in the best way possible. Next, remember that TV is a visual medium, so you must make your product visually appealing. Finally, presenting your product on TV shopping is a wonderful way to bring your story to life. This reminds me of being in school having "show-and-tell." Remember that? Well, the TV retailing world isn't any different, only now you're playing "show-and-sell."

Almost every product can be sold on TV, but some naturally excel more than others. For example, fragrances are nearly impossible to demonstrate on TV because viewers cannot actually experience the fragrance. So, be sure to determine if your product's features and benefits can be shown on TV. Does it show well, and is it demonstrable? In my experience, cleaning products, cooking appliances, apparel, and jewelry are easy to show. Most TV networks devote a sizable percentage of their precious airtime spread among these distinct categories. Also, cosmetics, hair care, and fitness equipment can be sold effectively with outstanding before and after visuals and amazing inspirational stories told by a credible personality. So, if a product isn't easily demonstrable visually, but you still believe you can sell it on TV, you must find a visual angle in your pitch before approaching any TV network.

Plus, knowing your product and its impact is essential because, during live TV sales, you have little time to tell a story before a response is needed. As I mentioned, everything on TV shopping is indexed by time measured by DPM. When I am on television, the network allows so much time, and as part of the deal, I must sell a certain amount of product per minute. The entire time, they monitor every sale, ensuring I hit my projected numbers. While the name of the game is to sell out, you also want to sell the most popular of your styles or products.

TV shopping channels are "shopping destinations," and people tune in regularly to watch and buy, so having a high-quality product that appeals to impulse shopping is ideal. Position your product in these channels, showing "the newness" for consumers to buy, inciting their desire for your product through personality, price, and story, creating a sense of urgency. Show the viewers how your product can help them by repeating and reiterating the problem and doing your best to shine much-needed light on how your product solves a problem. When your product solves a problem, magic happens. The viewer feels they must have it, which leads to large sales volumes.

Hit The Emotions through Benefits

To sell on TV, you must know everything about your product, but in particular, you must remember the all-important benefits that hit the buying emotions and make the phone ring. You must create an emotional connection between the viewer and your product. To do this, explain what your product does and how it will solve problems for your buyers or how it will improve their lives. The human brain is wired for emotional buying, and the concept of "retail therapy" has become a modern cliché backed up by scientific research. Here, the pleasure associated with shopping is attributed to dopamine delivered straight from our brains. Our neurotransmitters surge when we anticipate a reward, such as when we are tempted to buy something new.

The notion or hint of a sale gives us an even greater kick. When an unforeseen benefit enters our cognitive field, such as "30 percent off," dopamine spikes. It is common for people to buy something out of emotion and then justify it later with logic. When on TV, think about this scientific fact, and always consider appealing to your target customers' buying emotions rather than their logic.

Perfect Your Pitch—Stop Selling

I know it sounds counterintuitive, but you can sell more when you stop selling. No one wants to see a super salesperson turn on his "hard sell." Learning to connect emotionally with your audience is accomplished by openly sharing your vulnerabilities, capabilities, and unique story with your audience. For example, if your product is comfy but fashionable jeans, you can craft a story and presentation that might look like this: "I gained thirty pounds after I gave birth to my two children, and no matter how hard I tried to shed those extra pounds, I couldn't. The more I tried, the more weight I gained. Then, after menopause, I gained even more weight, and it got so bad that I gave up looking for a perfect pair of jeans that fit and were comfy and fashionable, not bulky and floppy. Finally, exhausted and disgusted with myself, I took matters into my own hands, designing that perfect pair of super fashionable and comfortable jeans that make my body look spectacular. Plus, I designed the jeans with stretch denim that runs with your body shape but remembers and retains its original shape. So, if you're tired of looking for that perfect pair of jeans or thought you couldn't wear jeans again because of a little bit of weight gain, give my jeans a try."

You can also make an emotional connection by sharing something you have in common with your audience. For example, say something like, "Thanksgiving (or any holiday) is just around the corner, and I'm sure you are looking forward to spending time with your family and friends. And in many ways, it's the most valuable time of the year, and I'm sure you'd want to share your best. My product helps you glow, sparkle, and look effortlessly polished for very little money." Of course, you can be as creative as you want in presenting your products. Still, the best way is to connect emotionally with your audience as soon as possible, using benefits supporting your brand and product messaging.

As part of the importance and power of the marketing message, you must present your product as easy to use and understand. So often many budding entrepreneurs miss the mark on their general message, and their presentation becomes muddled and confusing. Always remember that TV retailing is all about time, so your message must be communicated clearly, succinctly, and quickly in the most engaging way.

SETTLING IN FOR THE LONG TERM

When you finally reach the point where you can present your products to the TV network, remember, it's all about that particular professional buyer, playing the game, and shedding light on their accomplishments. The first thing you want to do is compliment the buyer and their efforts. Whether they buy for a department store, TV retailer (such as QVC), or an online store, professional buyers have difficult jobs. Yet, surprisingly, many still love their work despite the intensity and long hours. Retail environments are not always supportive, so buyers may appreciate affirmation. I usually tell my buyer how much I enjoyed watching a specific product sell out so quickly on television. The fact that you take the time to acknowledge their keen eye for a potential bestseller would be appreciated, even if it's one of your direct competitor's styles.

Spend more than half your appointment asking questions, but do not spend more time than necessary with them talking about yourself or your products. Instead, ask questions like, "What are some examples of your top sellers?" or "Is there a particular price range that works best for this product category?" Buyers are transparent if you ask the right questions, and vendors love to answer entrepreneurs' questions because it helps them build better products at better prices.

One of the best pieces of advice I can give you about television retailing is to be patient. The stakes are high, and there are risks, but the rewards can be even higher if you're patient. So, follow the steps and build and develop your TV retail campaigns. Be persistent, even though you may have the perfect product for TV and have vetted the TV network. Pause, do things properly, be creative, present professionally, learn the ropes, and watch your business soar to become your million-dollar passion. And lastly, by being patient and following the experience of others, your product or service can become a household name, benefiting millions of people, resulting in millions of dollars for the TV network—and most of all, for you.

KEY TAKEAWAYS

- Always be patient when pursuing TV retailers.
- Learn to connect with your audience emotionally.
- People tune in regularly to watch and buy, so have a great product that has appeal and encourages impulse shopping.
- Knowing your audience and determining who wants to buy your product is essential.
- Being in front of the camera and millions of viewers and shoppers, you can't risk having a lousy pitch person representing your products.
- Learn to craft a compelling story in sync with your product pitch.

CHAPTER 8

Eliminating Marketing Mayhem

*People don't buy what you do; they buy why you do it. And
what you do simply proves what you believe.*[1]

—SIMON SINEK

IT IS RARE FOR A MARKETING CAMPAIGN TO BE AS EFFECTIVE AS
the California Milk Processor Board's "Got Milk?" campaign. In
1993, Jon Steel, a partner at San Francisco–based advertising firm
Goodby, Silverstein & Partners, led a focus group to learn about
consumer's milk consumption in which he asked respondents to
not consume milk for a week before taking part in the discussion.
The concept "Got Milk?" revolved around the distress one feels
after running out of milk, and it turned into an ad that was featured for over two decades. There were seventy variations of this
commercial in California alone. What made this marketing and
advertising campaign unique when celebrity influence was at an
all-time high? And what was the driver that caused this marketing campaign to be successful? It was all because of planning and
extensive research.

I believe the marketing campaign was a massive success
because creators combined (compelling) copywriting, consumer
research, and influencer marketing to create an impactful series of

ads, which ran for more than ten years. The TV commercials and billboards hit home, connecting childhood feel-good emotions featuring Hollywood elites and celebrities, all proudly wearing a milk mustache. In a very subtle way, the ads invited everyone to drink more milk and proudly wear their milk mustache. It was brilliant marketing. From a marketing aspect, the key takeaway from this story is that marketing isn't advertising, and advertising isn't marketing. I majored in marketing, and I never took a class in advertising because it is such a small part of the overall umbrella of marketing, which includes: advertising; market research; identifying your core target audience; and forming an effective, multifaceted strategy with brand messaging.

I achieved marketing success through research and by clearly defining my target audience. Despite what the marketing gurus tout to most new or small business owners, my business grew without ever advertising on TV and I never spent a penny on infomercials or commercials. (When I appeared on TV shopping channels, I didn't pay for the time. They paid me, as long as my sales per minute were higher than their costs.) I've also never advertised my jewelry in fashion, jewelry magazines, or any other forms of print media. I never wanted to attract money partners or investors to grow my business. Yes, you can grow and build a million-dollar business unconventionally. However, every business enterprise can succeed only if it can keep its existing customers happy while attracting new ones, which is no small task. Every business enterprise has two primary functions for creating a customer: marketing and innovation.

Even in its most basic form, marketing is critical to any business. Marketing is all around you, with marketing messages surrounding your world as you know it, from your first memories to the moment before you even opened this book. Driving down the highway, you're inundated with marketing messages from road signs and billboards. When you stop for gas, premade marketing messages are played as you fill your car. Being constantly bombarded with marketing messages becomes the norm and consumers become complacent. To be successful, your marketing must make a massive impact with a fresh and innovative approach. Good marketing can change the culture and status of your new business, and as you build and grow, marketing will be an essential driver of your long- and short-term growth.

As a new business owner, you must first develop a plan. Be creative. Even with word-of-mouth referrals, your product or service will not market itself. While the mere mention of *marketing* intimidates most business owners (I understand because it is scary to do something you've never done), I promise it's easy to start. All you need to do is look at the marketing surrounding you. What do you see? Suppose you pay attention to the different tactics and strategies that engulf your world. Take your ideas from the marketing that draws you in and create your own innovative influence in the marketplace.

Marketing is highly subjective, and every business, large or small, needs effective marketing strategies to succeed. But what is marketing? Merriam-Webster's definition of marketing is "the process or technique of promoting, selling, and distributing a product or service."[2] While this sounds good in theory, from a more hands-on viewpoint, I would define marketing as "activities a company undertakes to inspire, offer solutions, and help elevate experiences of your product or service." In essence, the traditional definition says that "marketing" means putting your product in front of as many eyes as possible. My definition adds a new perspective, which helps you understand how important it is to market the likely outcome of using a product or service to your target market. Confusing marketing with advertising is a critical mistake many new business owners make. Advertising is a form of marketing, but it is only one aspect of the overall marketing picture. Here is a list of low-cost and effective marketing activities I've discovered:

- Networking
- Conducting Public Relations
- Blogging
- Maintaining an Effective Website
- Offering Enticing Promotions
- Conducting Ongoing Consumer Research
- Analyzing Competition
- Advertising
- Being Active on Social Media

Networking

Networking is the process of building strong relationships with potential and existing customers, partners, and other stakeholders to promote a product or service. This can be done through a variety of methods, such as attending industry events and trade shows, creating content on social media and leveraging your influencers to promote your brand. Networking is one of the strongest moves you can make as a marketer to increase your brand awareness and build relationships that can lead to increased sales and customer loyalty across the board.

Conducting Public Relations

Public relations are vital to your marketing strategy when spreading the word about your new business. For instance, public relations can help you maintain your reputation by gaining the approval of your audience, educating all potential consumers, and ultimately, helping them make informed purchasing decisions that include your products. In public relations, more detailed information is provided to the target market than would typically be provided through other marketing methods. For your company to shape its image, public relations are essential tools to support credibility and reputation. In addition, they are an excellent tool for generating attention if there is something newsworthy happening in your industry.

BLOGGING

Blogs are essential to establish your thought leadership and authoritative stance in your business and area of interest. Originally, blogs were primarily online diaries, where people wrote personal accounts of their lives. They've since grown to include writing and media on various topics, such as news, politics, music, food, and business, and there are even outstanding blogs on the subject and business of blogging. The blog format was recognized as a marketing tool by visionary entrepreneurs who used it to provide information and updates to their customers and to attract new clients. Over the years, blogging has developed into a new, fast-paced, intriguing, and compelling form of marketing.

Since blogs allow consumers and businesses to interact, they are ideal for marketing. Fortunately, most blogging platforms are easy to use and inexpensive to start and maintain. As well as supporting and building your website traffic, your blog can also give people a reason to repeatedly visit your website, enticing them to make a purchase.

Blogs, if done right, can improve your company's search engine ranking. Due to Google's (and other dominant search engine's) excellent ability to rank new content, many new entrepreneurs use blogging for search engine optimization (SEO). Blogging is also a good way to gain trust and credibility with your target audience and potential new customers. You can demonstrate that you are an expert in your field, provide helpful tips, and deliver other valuable information with a blog so consumers feel confident in your product or service. In addition, with a continuous blog campaign, you can encourage readers to sign up for email lists or promotional offers or contact you for more product information.

CHAPTER 8

Maintaining an Effective Website

In today's business world, it may seem as if everyone has a website, and most of us have become complacent with their upkeep. The power of an effective website cannot be overstated. Online information helps consumers make better purchasing decisions, and your website plays a crucial role in capturing and retaining customers. According to the eCommerce Foundation, 88 percent of consumers research products before purchasing.[3] This buying behavior trend underscores the importance of having a website. Your website is your business's backbone, supporting all your online and offline marketing efforts, and it is a place for your customers to learn more about you and your products. Not only does your website help you build credibility and authority, but it also helps you distinguish yourself from your competitors. Websites also benefit brick-and-mortar businesses that serve mainly local customers, by giving your customers a clear idea of what types of products or services you offer. Millennials are so comfortable with their mobile phones that even when they are in a physical store, they often check out the brand's website to see if new colors, styles, or prices are available. Your website can make a positive impression on your potential customers and keep your loyal customers interested in your products.

Offering Enticing Promotions

A business's marketing and promotion efforts work together to attract new customers and increase sales. You need to understand the basics of promotion to be successful in business because, without promotion, it is impossible to bring a new product to market successfully. Promoting your company's products, concepts, or ideas means combining various activities to inform potential consumers about the product's merits and to stimulate their desire to purchase it.

By describing a product and its characteristics, promotion creates synergy and enthusiasm from buyers to purchase your product. Your company's promotion plan usually allocates separate goods and services to push consumers from a state of awareness to actually buying your product. Additionally, you can promote your business and showcase your beliefs by participating in local life, positively impacting society, being a proponent of an issue that is important to you, or joining in a particular cause.

CONDUCTING ONGOING CONSUMER RESEARCH

Through the power of consumer research, you can gain a deeper understanding of what drives customer behavior and what delivers results. The term *consumer research* if often misunderstood. Conducting consumer research means listening to and understanding your customers through qualitative and quantitative fieldwork. Simply put, it is getting to know customers' opinions, attitudes, behaviors, and needs by talking to them. Consumer research refers to the collection and analysis of this consumer data.

You can conduct consumer research in various ways, including launching large-scale online surveys, sponsoring focus groups, conducting face-to-face interviews, and offering workshops. Besides developing marketing activities and strategies, consumer research can also spawn propositions and products, branding strategies, advertising campaigns, and public relations campaigns.

ANALYZING COMPETITION

Analyzing and understanding your competition, evaluating their strengths and weaknesses, allows you to determine how you can compete in the same market. The primary goals of a competitor analysis include:

- identifying the strongest competitors;
- analyzing the strategies of competitors;
- predicting their behavior;
- anticipating their reactions; and

• influencing their actions in your favor.

With this information, you can create, implement, and adjust strategies to improve your business's efforts and identify potential threats. Businesses conduct competitor analysis at various stages based on impressions, conjectures, and intuition to ensure all possibilities and actions are considered.

ADVERTISING

Advertising, promotions, communications, and sales are all tools to execute effective marketing strategies. However, there is more to marketing than meets the eye with advertising.

Many small business owners believe that advertising equals promotion or marketing as a primary tool to increase visibility. In fact, they all work together to create a strong sales strategy. There are many advertising and marketing strategies that you can employ for your business, including word-of-mouth advertising, networking, blogging (including guest bloggers), and do-it-yourself public relations.

Word-of-mouth advertising is the most organic and healthy way to grow your business. Yet many entrepreneurs shy away and do not focus on this powerful strategy. In modern marketing, entrepreneurs have access to numerous tools for word-of-mouth marketing. You can create a community for your customers on your website, or create a separate URL for your community. You can also develop a community on social media where your customers can share experiences and stories. Ask for testimonials or referrals after every sale and develop a follow-up system to reach customers after the sale, keeping them talking about your business and keeping your product fresh in their minds. Implement a rewards program for new customers and anyone who shares and introduces your company to a new potential customer. And there isn't anything wrong with asking your customers to share your web page and social media pages with others on the Internet. Ask others to help you organically grow exponentially without spending hundreds of thousands of dollars.

The importance and power of networking for small business owners cannot be overstated. You can network with companies in similar but noncompeting industries in your community. For instance, if you run a yoga studio, you might want to network with businesses involved in nutrition, weight loss, skincare, and hair care. If you own a pet store, you can network with veterinarians, pet hospitals, groomers, and local and national kennels. With the power of the Internet, networking can also be done with local and international business owners worldwide.

Another cost-effective marketing strategy is guest blogging, which is the practice of writing and publishing a blog post on another person's or company's website. Usually, guest bloggers receive credit for their posts along with a link to their websites and product offerings. You can use guest blogging to build relationships with others in your industry, expose your brand to new audiences, and drive traffic to your website. At the same time, establish yourself as a thought leader, and build backlinks that may boost your search engine rankings. If you want targeted traffic to your blog, high search engine rankings, and a more substantial reputation in your niche—all for free—guest blogging is one of the best strategies to employ. You can begin by pitching yourself and your topic to relevant websites with audiences in your industry. Then, ask permission to write a blog in return for links to your landing page or website. The advantage of writing a blog on someone else's site is that you get exposure to all their customers as well as your own.

BEING ACTIVE ON SOCIAL MEDIA

Social media offers businesses a significant cost-effective advantage and allows easy access to nearly all potential customers. But, contrary to what everyone touts and believes, social media is not an effective tool to sell your products or services without a strategic social media marketing plan. Social media is a tool that allows you and your brand to building a following. While you *can* sell your products or services on social media, you must understand thoroughly what each social media platform is about in order to target your marketing effectively. As a small business owner, you must be active on social media platforms where your ideal customers engage in large numbers. Maximizing your efforts will take experimenting and thorough research on each platform. I will explain each platform to help you decide which route to take. Admittedly, social media did not exist in 1989 when I started my business, and when early social media platforms such as Facebook did appear on the market, I did not initially embrace them. Yet, once I applied myself, the sky was the limit to the power and leverage afforded by using social media. Building a social media following takes time, effort, creativity, and sometimes money. But in the end, it is well worth the effort. Before using any social media platform for your business, you must explore each one and weigh the pros and cons, ensuring your marketing is in sync with the platform you're marketing on.

The mistake I witness many new entrepreneurs make is trying to follow and grow every social media platform when not every social site suits their product or service. Your marketing will not be effective by doing this because it is impossible to build a significant following on all social media platforms unless you are already a mega-celebrity. To gain a strategic advantage, you must understand the strengths and weaknesses of each social media platform you intend to use.

Facebook

Facebook's primary advantage over other social media platforms is that its platform is relationship focused, connecting the users' family and friends. Facebook has been the world's largest social media platform for years, with well over two billion users. With Facebook's extensive appeal and reach, you can easily turn your client base into a community. Your business can have a Facebook page where you encourage your customers to connect with other product users. You can post testimonials as well as appealing behind-the-scenes pictures.

Furthermore, you can let your followers know about new products and services. You can offer them a sneak peek to create excitement and buzz before a new product launch. Facebook also makes it incredibly easy to start a business page and an account within their platform. Also, you can use Facebook to cross-promote fresh content on your website by using your posts, videos, photos, and contests. Despite its benefits, Facebook has some drawbacks. First, its users tend to be older, ages forty-five to sixty-five, so investing time and effort to build a Facebook following is not advised if your product appeals to younger demographics, such as millennials.

Instagram
Instagram was initially designed for raw, unfiltered photos of the moment. Despite its relative youth, Instagram's growth has been exponential, with over one billion users. Instagram is known for photos and short videos, and its demographics skew to younger audiences than Facebook—a significant percentage of their users are millennials, especially millennial moms. So for brands targeting young, hip demographics, Instagram is the best social media platform, primarily if your business focuses on beauty, travel, food, and fashion. On the platform, short videos and photos with short texts perform well.

However, one of the disadvantages of Instagram is that you need decent photography skills to succeed. Instagram doesn't give you much space to describe your photos outside of captions.

YouTube
YouTube is the premier educational social media platform, with approximately two billion users. You can use it to show how your

products are used and can promote your brands with inspirational backstories about you and your products. It is an excellent platform for you to visually differentiate your products from your competitors'. You can even show how your products are designed and manufactured behind the scenes. This makes the content engaging and supports your brand.

What are the best ways to use YouTube to reach your audience? There are several options available. You can create instructional videos, product reviews, and other content for your target market. YouTube also boosts your visibility since your videos appear in Google search results, allowing you to cross-promote your content across different social media platforms. However, YouTube's biggest drawback is that in order to truly gain traction, you must consistently produce high-quality, entertaining, and informative videos.

TikTok

One of the newest platforms to hit the US market is TikTok. And according to Sandvine, a network intelligence company, online video traffic accounted for 65 percent of all consumers' Internet traffic in 2022.[4] It sounds crazy. Almost every social media platform has taken note of this trend, and with TikTok's rise, short videos dominate content creation. In many ways, TikTok makes it easy to build a huge following if you're willing to produce and post eye-catching videos constantly and consistently. In addition, TikTok offers branded channels for verified businesses that work similarly to YouTube by giving viewers one place to watch all the content your business wants to promote. Even if you aren't familiar with TikTok videos, the app's built-in creation tools make it easy to start. However, the downside is that this platform is primarily used by young users who do not yet earn an income. As a result, TikTok's conversion rate of conveying followers to customers is one of the lowest of all social media platforms.

LinkedIn

LinkedIn is exceedingly becoming the most effective social media platform for networking and professional contacts. The platform has approximately 610 million self-reported users, including employees and business owners across numerous industries. Unlike other social networks, this platform allows users to connect professionally and build professional relationships. And generally, LinkedIn users prefer business-to-business (B2B) content over business-to-consumer (B2C) posts, as you might expect. My experience has been that a company that markets directly to businesses does better on LinkedIn than one that markets directly to consumers. You can effectively reach the decision-makers and influencers of the business world through LinkedIn, so your chances of gaining recognition and getting a sale are higher.

The downside to LinkedIn is that it has fewer users compared to other platforms. Consequently, your reach there may not be as comprehensive as it would be on Facebook or Instagram. In addition, LinkedIn has less user interaction and engagement than other platforms and is *not* a B2C platform.

Pinterest

The word *Pinterest* is derived from two words, *pin* and *interest*. This company operates a photo-sharing website that is "the world's catalog of ideas" or a visual discovery, collection, and storage platform. I use this social media site and find browsing and searching for ideas and "pins" in my feed interesting. Pinterest has something for everyone and is beneficial for blogs and websites regarding business, and offers a high conversion rate for products such as food, clothing, jewelry, home décor, and more.

One of Pinterest's biggest advantages is that "pins" are essentially bookmarks that link back to an individual's or company's website. Pinterest has its pros and cons, just like every marketing platform. It's a highly visual platform with a more diverse user demographic than most other platforms, including Gen X, millennials, and even baby boomers. It's also a platform that can be used for promoting B2C and B2B content. Regarding Pinterest's disadvantages, its greatest strength can also be considered its greatest weakness: The entire platform relies on images. Therefore, you need to be careful about the images you post since it is the image that attracts followers. Be concerned and considerate of copyright issues and image quality. You will have people who follow you skip past your picture in their feed and not read your description if the pictures do not grab them.

Social media marketing involves advertising on the different social media platforms just discussed and engaging with users on those platforms. Setting your goals and itinerary is one of the first steps in implementing your social media plan, which should specify what you are trying to accomplish. You should also define goals and strategic objectives. By focusing on what you want to accomplish and knowing what targets to focus on, you'll know what to post where. Some social media goals might be to increase awareness of your brand, create involvement and engagement with your post and therefore your business, acquire leads that might result in sales, acquire customers, and measure traffic through your sites.

Once you know your goals, you'll need to determine your social media budget, and then spend it wisely, whether the currency is time or advertising. In other words, how much money should you spend? Your budget will determine some of your social media activities. For example, your budget will determine how many organic and paid campaigns you can run simultaneously. Also, depending on your budget, you can use various social media tools to make your tasks more productive. Having said that, having a low budget is not necessarily a bad thing. However, you should be aware of this to structure your campaigns accordingly.

For your social media marketing to be effective, you must define and create a buyer persona. Even the best marketer will achieve poor results if they target the wrong audience. That's why understanding your ideal buyer is so important. Your buyer persona should include details such as name, age, income, gender, location, what problems your products alleviate, dreams and ambitions, interests, past purchase patterns, and channels they use most on social media. Include all these demographics in your social media plan and do everything within your reach to gather every detail you can on your target customer and audience.

DO-IT-YOURSELF PUBLIC RELATIONS

A do-it-yourself public relations (PR) campaign accomplishes similar goals and objectives as hiring a professional PR agency, but without the extraordinary cost. Do-it-yourself PR is about getting attention and influencing your audience, whether you use press releases, magazine features, or social media posts. But is do-it-yourself PR a good fit for everybody? PR isn't something many people would choose to handle on their own if they had the option. It used to be an area with only a handful of elite marketing and public relations agencies who were super-connected to editors and producers of print magazines, newspapers, radio shows, and TV channels. The PR business, however, has become exponentially fragmented and diluted with the advent of the Internet. Thousands of outlets are looking for small business owners like you for inspirational stories, demonstrations on how to solve everyday problems, and more. The most important thing about do-it-yourself PR is that you must have a focused strategy and be persistent, but patient. Getting the proper visibility for your business is one of the most impactful activities you can do to grow your business. So, what does it take to master PR for your business?

You must understand your target audience. For example, you wouldn't want to pitch a crime show producer a story about wedding dresses. Instead, you might approach editors of bridal magazines. Once you've identified a target audience of editors and radio and TV shows, start listening to and watching those shows.

In other words, make sure you do your research about the show so when you do engage them in a quality dialogue, you can start with something like, "I watch your show regularly and especially loved the episode. . . . " Continue to engage in a short, professional dialogue before pitching them. Pitching thought-provoking ideas and measuring results against your objectives are the keys to successful do-it-yourself PR.

Reporter Access

Every day, reporters, editors, and producers look for stories that will interest their audience. However, there are just as many, probably more in fact, businesses and organizations looking to provide those stories, so the competition is steep, and the name of the game is access. One great way to gain access to reporters from all over the US is an organization called Help a Reporter Out (HARO). It can be found at www.helpareporter.com, and nearly all major news media outlets use it to find expert sources. A bulletin of needs is delivered several times a day via email. It covers multiple topics, including health and beauty, personal finance, mind and body, medical experts, education, and more.

Do Your Research

Creating your own PR will take effort and arduous work, and it all starts with research. First, start watching TV programs and listening to radio shows you'd like to be featured on. Next, subscribe to newspapers and magazines in which you'd like to be featured. Next, note the names of the writers and reporters in specific periodicals you wish to reach out to. Finally, when you contact your intended list of people, tell them why your expertise or story is an excellent fit for their audience by referencing specific articles or stories they've featured in the past.

Build Relationships with Editors

Use the information you learned from your market and editorial research and contact those editors, informing them of who you are and what you do, and how you can help their audience with your expertise. The editors love new angles on popular topics or stories that haven't been covered by their organization yet. Be persistent and patient, as editors and producers receive hundreds of inquiries weekly. Don't be surprised if you don't hear back from them the first time you contact them. Instead, write to them again when you have a timely or interesting story that fits their editorial calendar. For example, for Women's History Month in March, you can pitch editors about how you are a woman who started your own business or about your female ancestors who inspired your company's founding.

Product or Service Press Release

Crafting a press release to announce the launch of a new product or service aims to promote the launch as a newsworthy event and ensure that the media will cover it. Your go-to market strategy should include one, and it should be on your product launch checklist. A press release should focus on the product, specifically, what type of problems it solves, how your product solves them, who you are, and where readers can find the product. Be sure to list your company contact information so that editors and producers can contact you for more information.

CONSUMER MARKETING TOUCHPOINTS

It's important to vary your marketing strategies across several mediums and platforms. Consider that a customer must experience several "touches," that is, consumer marketing touchpoints that quickly nudge potential customers and help influence their purchasing decision, before buying something. This is also known as "breadcrumb marketing," where you're dropping "crumbs" your consumer can track back to your intended product, which could drive traffic to your brick-and-mortar store, website, or online store. Or perhaps a touchpoint may be used to alter and solidify brand perception to consumers. It may seem counterintuitive to what you've been taught because, traditionally, most of us have been hit over the head about ads, TV spots, radio advertisements, and direct mail pieces that should be used to tell the entire story—in one sitting. But today's consumers shut down with pushy sales tactics or ads. This is where social media comes into the marketing picture. Due to its low cost and inherent limitations, such as Twitter's character limit, social media is ideal for brief and limited breadcrumb and touchpoint navigation. You don't have to tell them the whole story in one go; the key is to leave them wanting more with every post, interaction, and email you send.

And after launching many marketing campaigns, through trial and error, I've found that touching a potential customer must happen approximately five to thirty times before purchase. The ideal number of touchpoints depends on the product type and price point. For example, a luxury automobile costing $100,000 would require more touchpoints than a new cookware set. Touchpoints can include face-to-face interaction (if you run a physical store), social media posts, newsletters, emails, how-to videos, website landing pages, free PR, and other ways to engage your potential customer. In many companies, marketing uses various touchpoints to enhance the customer experience. Consumer touch points are vital, influencing multiple factors related to sales, customer satisfaction, and brand image. In addition, those touchpoints encourage repeat purchases from existing customers.

One critical aspect of touchpoints is understanding how to touch your customers *after* the sale. For example, operating instructions and spare parts manuals are now often only offered electronically, and most customers expect to obtain them via your company website specifically for this purpose. The documents can be accessed at any time and cannot get lost. Making a website landing page for these documents is an excellent place to advertise and touch your customer after the sale. Even a company newsletter or mailer is an ideal after-sale touchpoint, along with your email signature. The variants mentioned here are good starting points for further consideration of the customer touchpoints in after-sales.

Marketing is not complicated and is primarily based on common sense. However, you must be prepared to do the work and commit to the cause. Marketing is the ever-present constant in your business, and you must be in it for the long haul because to grow your business, you must engage in all aspects of marketing your products and business to achieve the status you desire.

KEY TAKEAWAYS

- For your social media marketing to be effective, you must define and create a buyer persona.

- If you follow the do-it-yourself route, marketing doesn't have to cost much money.

- Marketing plans identify the target market, the value proposition of the brand or product, the marketing campaigns to be implemented, and the metrics to be used to assess marketing success.

- Metrics that show which marketing efforts have an impact should be used to adjust the marketing plan continuously.

- The results of digital marketing are visible in near-real time, while TV ads require rotation to achieve any level of market penetration.

- A business marketing plan describes a company's essential aspects, such as its goals, values, mission statement, budget, and strategies.

CHAPTER 9

Effective Pricing Strategies

Price is what you pay. Value is what you get.[1]

—WARREN BUFFETT

THE PRICE TAG, WHEN IT WAS INVENTED IN THE 1870S, ALLOWED companies to scale their pricing to more complex assortments, eliminating the need for shopkeepers to remember every product's price. All retailers needed to do was decide on a price for each product, add a price tag, and return to the old Quaker model in which stores charged the same price for every product, regardless of who bought it. It's hard to imagine a world without price tags after this model became standard. Almost universally, price tags have dictated how we interact with retail stores for 150 years. Many people don't care which retailer they buy a product from as long as they get it at a fair price. Price tags and the pricing of a product or service are important for every business, large and small.

Pricing is an art, science, and certainty in the business world; it is the heart and core of your business, and if your products or services are priced well, they will sell well. If not, it can lead to troubled waters. Businesses of all sizes and stature need a pricing strategy, but small business owners need it more than anyone else because their businesses will ultimately fail without one. Katherine Paine said it best, "The moment you make a mistake in pricing, you're eating into your reputation or your profits."[2]

Effective and strategic pricing is the most critical component to maximizing your revenue for the long term and is a significant factor in building your brand and business reputation. For example, when I began my jewelry company, once I discovered my niche, I focused on affordable strategic pricing, dancing a fine line between elegance and affordability, and maintaining the premium quality jewelry for which I was known—providing premium quality products at affordable prices resonated with my customers because of their perceived value. Because of this pricing model's remarkable success, I have stuck to it. But the one key aspect was that I never used the words "lowest prices." My prices were not the lowest, but neither were they the highest. Instead, I found balance—the focal point that resonated with the customer, driving sales beyond my imagination.

Alexander Turney Stewart, an Irish immigrant in the 1840s, thought there was a better way to buy popular goods than the popular auctions practiced in the day. However, it was his ingenious idea to create a store that posted prices with one caveat—no haggling allowed. In this way, buyers and sellers were less likely to be dissatisfied with auctions, while business owners maximized profits from each purchase. It has exploded since then and now dominates all commerce for more standardized products. Since the debate and haggling were removed from the sale, companies were left to figure out how to price their products, leaving room for error. To address this, many businesses have discovered three pricing options chosen by many businesses worldwide:

- Cost-Based
- Value-Based
- Dynamic

Cost-Based

Manufacturers typically use this pricing type since it requires the least amount of consumer information. Creating the product is simply a cost, plus a percent markup toward wholesale and other distribution methods.

Value-Based

A value-based pricing strategy optimizes a product's perceived value to the consumer. For high-end, trendy, name-brand products or even something consumers can't live without, it's ideal. Have you ever been to a fair or an outdoor festival when the weather was blazing hot? Chances are you needed a cold, refreshing drink, so you gladly paid the high price vendors were asking. This is a value-based principle at work. The cost of the product sold does not correlate with value-based pricing. Instead, this pricing is based on the monetary value your customers place on the product.

Dynamic

Because of the rapid advancement of technology, dynamic pricing has taken off in the last decade, as it combines algorithms to maximize economic welfare and profits. This is because knowing how many sales each price point generates is essential to measuring economic welfare. And because the consumer has the choice to buy or not buy the product. Using pricing strategies like this has become increasingly popular, as they benefit both sides of the sale and are ideal for industries such as airlines, hospitality, and e-commerce. Even though so much progress has already been made in the pricing field, there is still much more to the whole pricing picture. Studies have found that a 1 percent improvement in your pricing can add up to 11 percent in profits.[3] Of course, with incorrect pricing, you're missing profits. The trick is finding the happy medium between high pricing with a touch of snob appeal and low pricing that causes doubts about the quality of your product. The dynamic pricing model depends heavily on advanced technology using state-of-the-art algorithms, which must be monitored as often as every fifteen minutes.

Developing a Pricing Strategy

Developing an effective pricing strategy at the onset will help you and your business reach the level and goals you intend to achieve. When considering an effective pricing strategy, evaluate these factors:

- Brand Positioning
- Perceived Value
- Minimum Gross Margin Requirements

Brand Positioning

Your brand's positioning must be perfectly aligned with your pricing. When the product price is high because of high quality and exclusivity, and the brand positioning emphasizes these factors, the price automatically becomes reasonable in the eyes of the customers. But if the pricing of your products is too low, it may hurt not only your brand positioning and perception of your company but also your gross margins and ultimately your profits. For example, say you take your spouse to a fine dining establishment for your anniversary, but the restaurant offers a steak and lobster dinner for only $5. Would your spouse see the meal as a real-valued saving, or would they believe you are cheap and do not value the anniversary? Moreover, you and your spouse might question the quality of the steak you are about to consume. The same goes for your own pricing—low pricing can make consumers judge your brand of goods and services, lessening the actual value.

Perceived Value

Top companies in most industries price their goods based on how their ideal customers perceive and value their products' features and benefits. Unfortunately, most business owners mistakenly focus their pricing strategy on cost-related criteria, often without regard to the product's value to the customer. In perceived value pricing, the business owner assesses the product's value according to each customer and charges a price based on the perceived value of the product's attributes. Consumers place a high value on perceived value, which includes the product or service itself, its quality, speed of delivery, product warranty, and social standing. You must clearly communicate your product's unique value proposition as a marketer. Imagine a builder marketing luxury homes in an upscale neighborhood. She might communicate all the features and benefits that elevate the perceived value of her homes, such as the safety of the newly created community, the quality of schools nearby, the country clubs or other social clubs, or the proximity to recreational activities such as proximity to both casual and fine dining options, easy access to freeways, an increase in social standing, as well as a multiyear home warranty against potential appliance defects.

Minimum Gross Profit Margin Requirements
Every business must set a minimum gross margin requirement to sustain and fuel its growth. If you do not understand this premise, here is a quick primer. A company's gross margin (also known as gross profit) represents the revenue it retains after subtracting its cost of goods sold (COGS). For example, a company with a gross profit margin of 45 percent keeps $0.45 of every dollar it makes. Because the cost of goods ($0.55 in this example) has been covered, the gross profits of the company can be channeled toward paying debts, general and administrative expenses, interest fees, lease payments, employee payroll, health insurance, business insurance, state and local taxes, and dividend distributions to yourself and any investors, if applicable, in your business. In addition, growth-minded entrepreneurs would need to set aside a certain percentage of their profits to fuel their company's future

growth, such as additional product development and hiring more personnel. Gross margin measures how production costs relate to your revenues. Putting this into perspective, if your company's gross margin is falling, you must cut corners to make ends meet.

Cutting employees, quality of materials used, or both could lead to employee burnout, damage to your company's reputation, increased exposure to product liability, and declining revenue. Instead, I would recommend a comprehensive, multifaceted, sustainable pricing strategy that includes the total value of all the features and benefits of your products and the perceived value your customers place on your products. Do not fall into the trap of setting low prices. It will result in a temporary lift in sales at best. For the long term, discounting your products will have catastrophic consequences. Instead, avoid offering low prices and be sure to include these costs within your pricing: raw materials, labor, packaging, shipping, customs duties (if any part of the product is imported), rent, staffing costs, insurance, and local and state business taxes.

DON'T COMPETE ONLY ON PRICE

When developing a business plan, most business owners mistakenly set their pricing strategy to match the lowest-price provider in the market. Many assume this is the only way to win business, but having the lowest price is not a strong pricing strategy for several reasons. First, even if you can actually be the lowest cost option for customers, it invites them to view your product or service as a commodity and obscures its value. Second, if the primary reason your customers discovered your company was due to your prices, you can bet they will leave you the minute they find a lower price option. In other words, you would attract customers who are only loyal to the lowest prices. Third, it's impossible to remain the lowest-priced company in the long run. Companies are constantly going bankrupt or discontinuing products, resulting in highly discounted prices, sometimes far below their actual cost of goods sold. Fourth, larger competitors with lower operating costs in niche markets may eventually enter your segment and destroy small businesses trying to compete only on price.

Here are several things to keep in mind as you set your prices.

Ceiling Price

The ceiling price is the maximum price you can charge for a product or service without experiencing a significant decrease in revenue. It can be determined by surveying experts and consumers and asking about pricing limits. However, it is essential to remember that the market's highest price may not be the ceiling price of your products.

Elasticity of Prices

In simple terms, price elasticity is a quantifiable measurement of changes in the product's demand in response to a change in price. Examples of relatively inelastic products are groceries and utilities. If prices of groceries increase, you will hear plenty of complaints, but consumers still need to eat. They may be more careful about managing their dietary needs, but groceries are relatively price inelastic. For example, increasing the price of a gallon of milk from $2.00 to $2.50, a 25 percent increase in price, would not result in a 25 percent decrease in milk consumption. Likewise, increasing the price from $2.00 to $4.00, a 100 percent price increase, would not result in a 100 percent decrease in milk consumption. Sure, a 100 percent price increase would cause *some* reduction in consumption, but not 100 percent.

An example of products subject to high price elasticity is restaurants. Imagine what would happen to your neighborhood restaurant if it raised its menu prices by 100 percent. As a new marketer and business owner, you must understand how elastic and sensitive your products are to fluctuations in price when contemplating how to set or change a price. If your products are highly price elastic, you can reduce your prices slightly to generate significantly higher revenue.

STRATEGIC PRICING STRATEGIES

In the first phase of your entrepreneurship journey, it might be difficult to know if you are implementing strategies that will help you build a brand, maximize your product's profit potential, and still be competitively priced within your product category. Doing this successfully takes research, trial and error, and test pricing that moves your product or service up the ladder toward profit and success. However, pricing is something that even some of the most experienced CEOs and entrepreneurs struggle with. To remain competitive and maximize profits, your pricing strategies must evolve as the competitive landscape and consumer behavior change. The following pricing strategies are designed to help you gain the advantage.

Multitiered Pricing

You should offer, at a minimum, three-tiered pricing whenever possible. A prime example is the airline industry, the master of multitiered pricing. Most airlines provide multiple prices for the same flight based on certain variables, such as how much time in advance you purchase your ticket, the option to choose your seat, etc. The airline industry calls their pricing tiers "economy class, business class, and first class." Their multitiered pricing strategies have been successful, and they often sell out every seat on every flight. Some airlines have implemented even more tiers to their overall pricing strategies. For example, you might have heard of major airlines adding "premium economy, or economy comfort" class to their pricing. Hotels implement a similar pricing strategy, offering different prices for varying room options, such as court-yard rooms with no view, garden view rooms, and ocean or lake view rooms.

As a jewelry designer, I offer different price ranges for quality and design offerings. For example, a basic, simple collection of jewelry set in sterling silver would be priced the lowest in my collection. This is what I would call a "good" collection. On the other hand, the same designs set in 14K gold or 18K gold would be considered the "better" collection. In the "best" collection my consumers find diamonds set in 18K gold or platinum, incorporated with all the bells and whistles. All jewelry under the Victoria Wieck brand umbrella is made with expert workmanship and exceptional attention to detail. My customers can choose precisely how much money they want to spend and which features they value the most. Restaurants have also mastered the tiered pricing strategy by offering varying prices for single dishes, combination plates, and prefixed dinner specials. The beauty of the multitier pricing model is you can offer your customers exactly what they want and value, gaining what they will pay for without damaging your brand positioning, reputation, or profits.

Focus on Value

Focus on value, not price. If someone pays $5 for a pair of earrings to wear on Halloween and discovers that parts of the earrings became discolored after the first use, they didn't get a bargain, they got what they paid for. But if they paid $100 for a pair of 14K solid gold hoop earrings, they got a great deal because the earrings can be worn for an eternity, won't discolor, and will always hold their value. It's not products people buy but the results they'll get from them. Your product or service should be marketed regarding its value and benefits to your customers. Consider various ways to increase prices by adding additional value to your primary products. You might be pleasantly surprised at how much additional revenue you can generate by increasing your price to reflect an added value to your products. For example, a software company could add value by offering a technical support line for a limited time as well as a series of free online training programs. Or a clothing retailer may increase their prices when they introduce a new line made from sustainable materials. A move such as this could show added value that appeals to environmentally conscious consumers. Customization not only adds value, but it also helps customers feel special by having the ability to choose colors, design options, or monogramming. The perception of value is high if the customer believes they will get a lot for the price they pay. To be successful, you must create a high perceived value among your core customers. Consumers will pay more if they see more value in an item than its price tag. For example, TV networks positioned my jewelry brand as "luxury jewelry at affordable prices." It does not say "luxury jewelry at the lowest price." Throughout my twenty-five years of TV retailing, my jewelry brand has sold for about 30 percent more than the average jewelry price point on the network. For similar styles, I have outsold most lower-priced brands.

On one occasion, I had an item that cost me $17 and retailed for $79 because the network believed our customers would pay between $79 and $99 for that item, which was our customer's perceived value of this item. Despite having an extraordinarily high margin by their standards, they insisted on selling it for no less than $79 because it was our "better" item among the "good, better, best" pricing strategy that month. Their insight was dead on. We sold over twenty thousand units of this item in forty-eight hours. On the other hand, we had several items that cost us $120 to make, but we had to retail them for $259 to cover airtime, staff, packing, and shipping. When we priced this item at this higher price, it exceeded its perceived value, and we had no option but to discount it to make sales.

DIFFERENT PRICING MODELS AND STRATEGIES

As we have confirmed, very few factors impact a business's bottom line more than its prices. To help you better understand the semantics of pricing, I've evaluated some of the industry's most distinctive pricing models and strategies:

- Psychological Pricing
- Comparative Pricing
- Premium Pricing
- Cost-Effective Pricing
- Pricing Bundles
- Discounted Pricing
- Geographic Pricing
- Value Pricing
- Identical Pricing
- Context Pricing

Psychological Pricing

Let's begin with one of the oldest tricks in pricing strategists' guidebook—psychological pricing. Historically, psychological pricing was first used in the late 1800s. It involves pricing your goods and services below a nice, round number, to appeal to your customers' emotions. For example, rather than pricing a product at $100, you would price it at $99 or $99.99; a $25 item becomes $24.99. Round numbers are not standard. But what good is psychological pricing if every seller uses it and all customers are aware of it? The simple answer is because it works. Even though the price difference is negligible, potential customers see it as affordable, making them more inclined to buy. For you, this is the ideal outcome. Psychological pricing isn't for every business, because sometimes, a perception of a lower price can hurt sales, especially if your brand is premium and prestigious.

Comparative Pricing

Despite my criticism of businesses copying a competitor's prices, I do recommend that you research your competitors and their pricing and do your best to come close to, not copy, their pricing. Pricing your products higher or lower than your competitors' price points communicate to customers that you are a more premium or affordable company. In addition, there's a good chance your competitors have extensively researched and tested what prices your market responds to. So, using other companies' research to help you with your pricing and strategy can't hurt.

However, undercutting a competitor and using price as your primary tool to gain potential customers and their trust is wrong. Positioning your company as the low-cost option may squeeze margins to unsustainable levels. In addition, you might be attracting customers who value low prices over the features and benefits of the product. Keep in mind that you can also price your products above your competitors. Big brands have done this for decades. A higher price communicates quality, luxury, and prestige—three qualities your business wants to establish. Customers will become loyal to your brand if you compete on something other than the price. Finally, you can command a premium price if you build a premium-looking brand, even if your products are comparable to your competitors.

Premium Pricing
Many businesses use premium pricing as they begin or grow, setting their prices higher than the competition. While it may seem risky, premium pricing is successful in the early stages of a smaller enterprise product's life cycle or if your product is unique and one-off. For example, a business that produces high-quality goods and sells them to upper-class customers qualifies to use premium pricing. For this price approach to work, your brand must be positioned as the premium brand in your niche, with your products' high perceived value communicated. This is the strength of your brand with messaging that is appealing to your potential customers.

Cost-Effective Pricing

A cost-effective pricing strategy appeals to price-conscious customers, such as those with lower disposable incomes. Many retailers, such as Walmart and Costco, use this technique. Even many generic food manufacturers and distributors employ this pricing strategy to reduce marketing and manufacturing costs.

Pricing Bundles

The concept of pricing bundles refers to selling goods or services at a price lower than customers would pay if they bought them separately. By selling a variety of products bundled together at a lower price than if they were sold separately, you can get more money up front. You may also get your clients to fall in love with more than one of your products. It could be a win-win. When you bundle multiple products, you, the business owner, can save on shipping costs and multiple employees handling the same products if sold individually. Your customers win because they get to try several products while saving a great deal of money.

Discounted Pricing

To reward customers for certain actions, many brands modify the introductory pricing of their goods. These could include buying in bulk, paying early, and buying off-season in exchange for a discount. Aside from buy one, get one free (BOGO) offers, coupons, and discounts, there are many promotional pricing strategies. However, in many states and even nations, the price of a commodity must be held at its higher price for a certain period before it can be reduced. For example, in the US, many states require retailers to establish their regular retail price of products before putting them on sale. Therefore, if your products are sold at sale prices more than 50 percent of the time, the sale prices are considered regular retail prices, thus, you can't claim it as a sale price.

Geographic Pricing

Geographic pricing refers to pricing items or services according to their geographical location or market. For example, you can apply this technique when selling an item in a foreign country or when the economy or salaries differ between your country and the country where the buyer is located. And expenses associated with moving items from the point of origin to the point of sale are reflected in this pricing strategy because a lower fee may be charged if the customer's location is closer to the origination site. Higher premiums are charged to customers living in remote areas.

Identical Pricing

Have you ever experienced analysis paralysis and found yourself unable to decide between items to buy and ended up not buying anything? In the purchase decision-making process, most factors are subjective. For example, I may prefer one design over another based on my personal preference. However, one part of the buying process is entirely objective: the price. In a purchase, price is often the determining factor, and if I can't decide, I'll select the most affordable option. So will your customers. But understanding this is where you might encounter problems as a business owner. Why? Selling your products at the same price as your competitors will complicate the decision-making process for your customers.

Context Pricing

Context pricing refers to how comparison points influence buyers and contextual messages rather than actual price levels. In the same target market, identical products can sell at radically different prices when the context is strategically managed. Fast-food chains, for example, will offer coffee cheaper than upmarket cafes, such as Starbucks. But interestingly enough, the quality of the product could be the same.

Walmart, a master of contextual pricing, found they could charge a higher price for Pepsi and other cold beverages when they placed the product in the clothing aisle, not the beverage aisle. This example illustrates how context heavily influences pricing. The context of a purchase should influence its final price, but it doesn't in so many cases. Many factors influence pricing—not only the product itself—showing the power of contextual pricing.

PUTTING STRATEGIC PRICING INTO EFFECT

Assess your company's needs before deciding which tactics to use when pricing your products or services. You may experiment with different pricing techniques until you find what works best for your company. Along with pricing, you may also change your marketing strategy based on the market for each product or service. Bestselling author and business strategist W. Chan Kim wrote in his book, *Blue Ocean Strategy*, "The strategic price you set for your offering must not only attract buyers in large numbers but also help you retain them." Kim also stated, "Identify where the mass of target buyers is and what prices these buyers are prepared to pay for the products and services they currently use."[4] But remember, everyone is different, and you can't be everything to everyone. What appeals to one buyer may cause another to turn away.

Pricing your products is, at the core, one of the most critical components of your business's market strategy, and reaching and building a million-dollar business starts here. Choosing your pricing strategically, and coordinating it with your branding, marketing, advertising, distribution, placement, and, most of all, your people is the best plan to build your million-dollar enterprise.

The price of your products and services has a significant impact on the profit potential of your business. Gone are the days when business owners adopted a set-and-forget pricing strategy. It won't work; if you do this, you will leave considerable money on the table. As a new small business owner, you must avoid falling into this trap. Testing different pricing strategies is essential to your small business's bottom line and competitive edge, as your pricing strategy determines the market standard for your product or service. To achieve million-dollar success, follow your heart, be wise, and explore every pricing option available.

KEY TAKEAWAYS

- As small businesses lack economies of scale, they should avoid competing on price.

- Small businesses can avoid a price war by establishing their brands, offering niche products or services, and conducting active market research.

- Testing different pricing strategies is important to your small business's bottom line and competitive edge, as your pricing strategy determines the market standard for your product or service.

CHAPTER 10

The Fundamentals of Negotiating

Let us never negotiate out of fear. But let us never fear to negotiate.[1]

—JOHN F. KENNEDY

ON OCTOBER 30, 2013, THE WALT DISNEY COMPANY ANNOUNCED it had acquired Lucasfilm from founder George Lucas for $4.05 billion, evenly split between stock and cash. This was a lucrative deal, as the only shareholder of Lucas's company was him. Besides bolstering Disney's position as a leader in animation and superhero films, the Star Wars acquisition let it reap huge profits from its already lucrative media and merchandising business. As part of the privately negotiated deal, Disney promised to release Star Wars films every two or three years. In addition, the acquisition included a detailed script treatment for three of the films. According to Walt Disney chairman Robert Iger, a famous negotiator in Hollywood, this was an excellent deal for the sixty-eight-year-old Lucas, who sold his company after planning his retirement in 2011. Speaking of Lucas's decision to hand over his creative legacy to Disney, Bob Iger told the *New York Times*, "There was a lot of trust."[2]

This is an example of a favorable negotiation that worked out for George Lucas and for the Walt Disney Company, but not all negotiations fare as well. Negotiations may not go as well for various reasons, including lack of trust, miscommunication, and misunderstanding of the other party's needs. In addition, negotiations can fall apart due to an individual's inability to remain flexible and unwillingness to compromise. If one party has more power or leverage than the other, the uneven playing field makes it difficult to agree, hence the need to negotiate effectively.

The ability to negotiate is one of the most valuable and principal factors you need to possess to take your business across the finish line. My early days were filled with being the only young mom at the negotiating table, and I would often say, "If you don't accept this deal now, I'll bring my toddlers to negotiate on my behalf." The entire room would laugh because most people would agree that toddlers are excellent negotiators, even with their limited language skills. If you think about it, you probably had to negotiate with your parents, teachers, friends, and even with friends in school early in your life. Likewise, you negotiate with your colleagues, employees, employers, distributors, customers, tenants, and landlords in business. Unfortunately, business classes rarely cover this subject. If I had a magic wand, I would make "negotiating" a required course in school for teens as they prepare for the future.

Negotiating is not an art or a science, but a skill honed and practiced. Through practice, I have refined my techniques based on the who, why, what, and where of the negotiation. For example, even though our ultimate goals were the same, I dealt with HSN differently than I did with their Japanese sister network, honoring cultural differences. The negotiations were different because of where the companies were based. One thing I have never changed, no matter how I negotiate, or whom I'm negotiating with, is that I always focus on "their success." I want the deal to be successful for those with whom I am negotiating as well as for myself.

Negotiating surrounds us and we do it often in so many aspects of our lives, so you might as well be good at it. When developing a solid negotiation strategy, you should clearly understand your goals and objectives and what you envision receiving after the negotiation. You must also listen to the other party's position while remaining open to compromise to reach a mutually beneficial agreement.

Negotiating poorly can cost you opportunities, profits, prospective buyers, and trust as a small business owner. But successful negotiators can open new avenues, improve business relationships, increase profits, and improve work practices. And with these intense negotiations, you improve your life, reduce stress, and increase your chances of success in both business and personal life overall.

How do I know about negotiation? Beginning with a small Dallas jewelry wholesaler, I learned how to negotiate. I was young and unknown in the industry but was gaining traction. This particular company believed I needed their small order more than they needed my products. Being new, I gave up more in the negotiation than I wanted to, but I held firm, ensuring they didn't get *everything* they wanted. This was the beginning of my hands-on education that helped me negotiate with some of the country's largest and most notable retailers. I have piloted successful negotiations with retail giants such as Macy's, Saks-Fifth Avenue, Nordstrom, Neiman Marcus, HSN, ShopHQ, Jupiter TV Network in Japan, major airline inflight duty-free programs, airport gift shops, and major cruise line gift shops. I've negotiated deals worldwide, including countries in Asia, Europe, the Middle East, and South America. These negotiations were tough, educational, and often nail-biting, but they honed the skills I needed to achieve some of the most significant contracts of my career. The same will happen to you.

COMMUNICATION IN NEGOTIATION

Communication is critical in negotiation, especially for entrepreneurs and new business owners. As an integral part of the negotiation, communication must be well thought out and direct. Negotiation relies on effective communication between two or more parties to reach an agreement. The process involves understanding the interests of all parties and finding a solution that meets everyone's needs, following the following communication steps:

1. Identify the parties involved and their interests.

2. Clarify all the issues to be negotiated.

3. Gain an understanding of the other party's position.

4. Brainstorm and generate options.

5. Evaluate the options and select the best solutions.

6. Reach an agreement.

Throughout the process, maintain open, honest communication and be willing to compromise to reach a mutually beneficial outcome. A successful negotiation ends with each party feeling confident they met their goals. Every negotiation will have conflicts. For example, you may negotiate with your potential buyer because they want you to reduce your prices so they may increase their profits. What do you do? There are options other than lowering prices for both parties to feel they are getting what they desire.

Some options are negotiating payment terms or offering discounts for bulk orders. You can provide additional services or products to offset the price discount or agree on a more extended payment schedule to help your buyer. Some tactics include offering a longer warranty or flexible delivery times on your products.

Or maybe you are willing to incur the shipping costs at the higher price.

Good negotiation and communication involve certain elements that are essential and beneficial to the entire process when done correctly. I've put together the following list of advice:

- Negotiate in person rather than by email or other transmissions.
- Practice active listening.
- Practice makes perfect.
- Be authentically curious and ask questions.
- Show precisely how your products can help your customer.

Negotiate in Person Rather Than via Email or Other Transmissions

Many new business owners, especially small business owners, prefer to negotiate through email, text message, or even fax because it's safe and sometimes easier, but that's not the best route, and I believe doing it in those ways is simply a bad idea.

Negotiation should be done in person where ideas and concepts are less likely to be misconstrued, misunderstood, or even lost in translation. Negotiating face-to-face eases misunderstandings and allows you to see if your point is being conveyed accurately, increasing your odds of walking away with a successful deal.

Verbal communication efficiently conveys messages, while nonverbal cues add meaning and show emotions. Observing and interpreting nonverbal communication from the other party lets you better understand their feelings and sometimes their internal agenda. What is said, how it is said, and what is not communicated may all have hidden clues about what motivates the other party, and you don't get to see these clues over an email or other written communication. Over 50 percent of communication messages are nonverbal, such as body language.[3] Expert negotiators analyze body language during face-to-face negotiations, either in person or via video conferencing, and use it to their advantage.

Practice Active Listening

A skilled negotiator understands that active listening is vital to a successful outcome. Listening is more challenging than speaking in a negotiation. It requires patience and practice. Negotiations are based on what we hear and observe, so the more negotiation you partake in the stronger your ability to comprehend what is said (or not said) will be.

Practice Makes Perfect

Understanding the parts of skilled negotiation is vital, and you must commit to perfecting your skills. Negotiation is no different than learning to play a musical instrument or a sport. The more you do it, the better you will get, paving the way for success.

Be Authentically Curious and Ask Questions

Asking carefully framed questions will help you achieve better results in any negotiation. By asking the right questions, you can uncover facts, confirm assumptions, and uncover the other party's needs. For example, the first time I negotiated with HSN for a TV contract, I wondered why such a large company would want to negotiate with me, one of the smallest jewelry companies in the industry. I asked what they found appealing about me and my designs. My questions led to more questions, and their answers led to more questions. My ability to ask relevant questions politely and respectfully helped us reach a satisfactory agreement. Using skillful questioning can help you direct a negotiation toward your preferred outcome.

Show Precisely How Your Products Can Help Your Customer

The smart move in a negotiation is to educate customers or buyers about how your product or service benefits them. Even though it seems obvious, many businesses shy away from this area because of false assumptions, such as believing that an educated customer will be less loyal or know too much. Your customers need knowledge and insights that help them understand your products and how they can benefit from them. An evidence-based argument makes a remarkable impact and leaves a long-term impression on the audience.

MASTERING STEPS OF NEGOTIATION

If everyone thought like you, wouldn't the world be different? How would you feel if everyone spontaneously agreed to your wishes, thoughts, and emotions? Life does not work that way, so it would be wise to learn the art of negotiation.

Negotiations should occur on an equal playing field, with both parties performing due diligence and vetting each other before beginning. The only way to negotiate effectively is to achieve a win-win scenario for all parties involved. Below are the strategies I've formed from years of negotiating with some of the world's most experienced negotiators.

Establish a Relationship

In business negotiations with medium-to-large companies, small business owners usually deal with a legal department, buying office (usually the division's vice president), or even the president or CEO. It's smart to remember that these representatives are not negotiating with their own money, which likely means they have zero emotional involvement in the negotiating. To them, it isn't personal. However, the opposite is true for you as a small business owner. Everything is highly emotional, with your business often hanging in the balance. As a small business owner, you will endure primary emotions since your business is your livelihood and your passion. However, negotiations at a big-box retail level are never rooted in feeling or intuition; they are based on vetting your business, statistics, facts, and complex numbers derived from your sales data.

A wise negotiator establishes a relationship with the other party, working toward building mutual respect and trust. All business negotiations are based on trust, respect, and need. I have found that sharing your strengths and weaknesses is one of the best ways to build professional relationships. You cannot pretend your company is the best at everything in your product category. When I visited Dallas in 1989 for the first time, I told every wholesaler I had met my story. My business began with a bangles and tennis bracelets concept because I simply didn't have the money or resources to offer samples in other categories, such as rings and earrings. I believed that transparency was the best way to make the negotiations work. So I bravely asked for their feedback, assuring them it was my dream to make enough money to offer an entire jewelry line soon. It all came together as I explained the importance of delivering only the highest quality products; I was confident I could be the best in the tennis bracelets and bangles category. My plan worked. If you are open, sincere, and honest throughout the negotiation process, you will likely produce productive outcomes. As a businessperson and human, you are best positioned to negotiate when the other party likes, trusts, and respects you. Integrity, respect, and dignity are palpable qualities and the basis for a successful negotiation.

Focus on the Win-Win

A successful negotiation results in a win for both parties; if you think only of yourself during a negotiation, you will lose. The key to success is understanding what all parties need and working together to meet those needs. Be ready to lose if you only think of things as zero-sum games, which means the other party must lose for you to win. Here's an example from real life. Company X worked with Manufacturer Y in a business relationship as a primary subcontractor. Company X relentlessly and continuously demanded lower prices from Manufacturer Y. To accommodate price reductions, Manufacturer Y reduced their profit margins and cut costs, including personnel. Eventually, Manufacturer Y couldn't survive and closed, leaving Company X scrambling to find a new primary manufacturer. After experiencing revenue and profit declines for several years, Company X discovered its direct manufacturer was not easily replaceable. Neither side won. Ultimately, all parties involved should be on the same side of the fence to be a good negotiator.

Act Like an Adult

Remarkably, even high-level business deals come to a halt because one person thinks childishly, causing others to act the same way. You need to remember that everyone is out of balance when this occurs. So do your best to be the stable anchor, the respectable adult at the table, and help everyone stay on track. Staying calm and listening to what others are saying without interrupting, no matter how strange or ridiculous it may sound, is one method I've used successfully in these situations. Then I respond by saying, "Thank you for clarifying. According to what I heard you say, your team wants me to reduce my prices by 50 percent, deliver all products within four weeks of the purchase order, and charge you after sixty days instead of thirty. Is that correct?" I repeat everything I hear, letting them know their demands were heard and understood, asking for clarification respectfully. This often softens them enough to resume the conversation if things aren't ironed out to your satisfaction. As soon as that point arrives, you can discuss all topics on the table, usually starting with those you can agree upon first. Again, be calm and always search for points of agreement, even the smallest ones, to communicate effectively.

Respect the Rhythm

Negotiations are simply relationships with a rhythm. Respect it. Everything has its own rhythm, especially negotiations.

Sometimes it is best not to say anything and remember that silent pauses can be immensely powerful. Let yourself and others reflect on what has been said and don't rush for answers. Instead, do everything you can to sense the proper rhythm of everyone at the negotiation table, including yourself.

Recognizing these steps will help you master the art of negotiation. A good rapport with everyone at the table is essential to success. Besides creating an agreement, you are cultivating a long-term relationship and building your reputation.

When you master the art of negotiation, you will notice positive changes, primarily in yourself and your business. As you gain negotiation skills, you'll see the results in your work and the deals you close with greater confidence and ease.

AVOID COMMON MISTAKES

"Negotiation" is a term commonly associated with business transactions and deals and is one of the essential parts of business communication and leadership. In order to be an effective negotiator, you must avoid the following common mistakes:

- Not doing enough research
- Failing to be flexible
- Not setting clear goals
- Not asking questions
- Not preparing for the negotiation
- Involving lawyers prematurely

Research everything you can about the parties you will negotiate with before entering a negotiation. For example, if the company is publicly held, you can learn about its size, revenue goals, profit margin goals, customer profile, company culture, and core mission. Discovering the company's "nonnegotiables" before negotiating is also intelligent and savvy. The more you know, the more powerful your negotiating skills become.

It also pays to be flexible. The rigidity of a negotiator's approach may prevent them from reaching a mutually beneficial conclusion. So being open to alternatives and willing to compromise is essential.

Also know what you want when you sit down at the negotiating table. Negotiators without a clear idea of what they want to achieve will probably make concessions they may regret later.

Negotiators who don't ask questions or seek clarification on specific points may not understand the other party's position or needs and could miss an opportunity to craft a deal that meets both interested parties' needs.

And last but not least, do not make any assumptions about the deal or who you are dealing with. What you think is vital to the other party may not matter to them. One of the most common mistakes negotiators make is not thoroughly preparing. You will probably leave value on the table if you do not conduct analysis and research. The other party may even exploit you if you have not done the research. You can prevent this scenario by developing a negotiation preparation checklist specific to your company and business that helps you think through your position, the other party's position, and what might happen.

Some of your preparation will not seem relevant, and new issues and problems will arise and require your attention during business negotiations, but here are several questions you need to ask yourself that will get you started:

- What are my short- and long-term negotiation goals?
- What are my strengths: values, skills, and assets as a negotiator?
- Which weaknesses and vulnerabilities do I have in this negotiation?

- What does the other party want or need from me?
- What are the issues I am ready to compromise on?
- What is the worst that could happen if I disagree?

When to Bring in the Lawyers

An excellent legal counselor is essential for every startup founder. The term *legal counselor* is used instead of *attorney* because when starting a business, you need someone to guide you rather than a hard-nosed attorney who will fight for you. Although attorneys are a necessary part of doing business, it's my experience that once an attorney gets involved, all negotiations stop until the other party involves their attorney. Things grind to a halt, making each party unable to communicate further. I advise against involving your attorney early, although nothing is wrong with it except that most attorneys do not understand your business's needs as well as you. Instead, I recommend bringing in attorneys after all business issues have been resolved. We rely on attorneys to draft agreements and prepare filings per the law. As your business evolves, attorneys can help you put your initial business agreements in a legal format that can withstand any legal challenges that might arise. Unfortunately, many small business owners abdicate decision-making authority to their lawyers, leading to lost deals, strained relationships with investors or customers, and less than optimal deal terms.

No matter how remote a risk or pitfall may seem, lawyers are trained to identify it. It's their job to alert us to potential problems. But as a new business owner, filter that information, apply the perspective, and evaluate risk versus reward trade-offs. Attorneys are not decision-makers—they are counselors. Your attorney should never be responsible for your decision-making process.

Advantages of Legal Representation in Negotiations

Lawyers can provide invaluable assistance during a negotiation if brought to the table at the right time. They can provide a level of objectivity that may be difficult to achieve otherwise. Also, a lawyer can help ensure you know your legal rights and obligations and protect your interests in any agreement you enter, as well as ensure that those agreements are legally binding. Lawyers can also guide you on discussing issues that may arise during negotiations and alert you to any potential legal risks. Anything you can do early to prevent such risk will be invaluable, as lawsuits can cost you money, time, effort, and, most of all, your reputation.

Disadvantages of Legal Representation in Negotiations

I want to dispel a long-standing myth about attorneys and negotiations. Somewhere along the way it was believed that attorneys needed to be brought in to help the negotiation because they had the skills to complete the transaction, and they would do a better job. I do not necessarily agree.

Every company I've done business with comes to the table with varying payment terms, specific shipping requirements, gross margin requirements, and product return rates. These are all challenging parts to understand, and it would cost a fortune to have your lawyer explain them to you. Instead, I suggest you educate yourself by performing research, talking to staff, and networking with other people to gather the information you need.

Bringing an attorney into a negotiation too early can be counterproductive, create an adversarial atmosphere, and send a message to the other party that you're not open to compromise. At the onset, negotiating without an attorney can be more effective. It allows for more open dialogue between you and the other party, allowing you the space and freedom to agree. Most attorneys are specialized, trained in "legalese," and understand courtrooms, but most are not trained as businesspeople. Among all professions, attorneys are some of the most risk averse. Every day, entrepreneurs must take calculated, measured risks to succeed. Why explain to your attorney your specific business model, the risks you will take, what issues you are willing to compromise on, and why some issues are more important than others when you can just do the job yourself?

I remember my first negotiation. I had to update my lawyer on the deal and who I was dealing with. Doing my due diligence, I asked my attorney to do his homework and compile information on the other party, including but not limited to their typical payment terms, their specific quality control requirements, and anything else they require from their vendors. They got to work, and once I set this in motion, the clock was ticking. They billed me per hour, racking up an astronomical bill of around five to ten thousand dollars weekly. This is not unusual for a lawyer. The average attorney charges hundreds of dollars per hour. A few attorneys I've worked with charge over $1,000 per hour and may require a monthly retainer before taking on a new client. Attorneys get paid despite the outcome of the negotiations, and don't have the financial risks you do.

Lawyers can complicate negotiations by introducing legal jargon and drawing out negotiations, consuming a lot of unnecessary time. Lawyers can also diminish your ability to establish a level of respect, trust, and honesty with the people you hope to make a deal with. Lawyers will keep negotiations impersonal, which is relatively routine and the norm for large corporations, but not ideal for small business owners.

Attorneys are always necessary and ideally suited for their role but should only be brought in to ensure everything is above-board with the negotiation details after you and the other party have come to terms and done everything you could do.

How Negotiations Work

Now that we've established the reasons strong negotiation skills are necessary, and reviewed the mistakes that can be made, let's examine precisely how negotiations work. In negotiations, two or more parties communicate to find an acceptable solution that meets the respective needs and interests of all parties. During any negotiation, the goal is for everyone to walk away with a fair deal. Through various techniques, including offers, bargains, and compromises, the goal is to reach a mutually beneficial agreement that is fair and equitable for all parties involved. It's important that each party has an equal say and stance. In a negotiation, you may identify the other party's issues, and they may present their position. There's an ebb and flow to the process. The other party then decides to either accept the proposed offer, counter it, or reject it all together and submit a different offer. This procedure repeats until all parties arrive at a resolution. Negotiation is like the game of chess—it's not complete rocket science, but it is an art. As with any game of skill, you must understand the rules in order to play well, which will reduce your apprehension and allow you to enjoy the process.

Set Realistic Options

What do you want to gain from your negotiations? Before entering into any negotiation, write all the issues you want to negotiate in the order of priority. Without a goal in mind, you're likely to lose your way and time and effort you spend will prove fruitless and wasteful. It is crucial to have a specific outcome in mind before starting any discussion.

Once the initial positions are clarified, it is important to realize that agreeing to them may not be possible. Usually, after you present your first offer, the other party will present alternative offers. Therefore, time is well spent to determine if there is any flexibility in the party's offer. In such situations, you must be flexible and work diligently to find substitutes and alternatives everyone can live with. And don't be shocked when, after weighing the pros and cons of each alternative offer, both sides end up happier with the alternatives than with the opening offer. By performing

CHAPTER 10

due diligence, both sides have gained and received information not initially available. In addition, compromises and concessions contribute to developing trust between the parties and influence their working relationship.

Commitment Level

In negotiating, considering how committed the parties are is vital to a successful outcome. One party's stake in the outcome may be significantly higher than another's, making them more interested and more determined to find solutions. The outcome of a particular negotiation with a large corporation capable of issuing large and lucrative contracts might be life-changing for a small business owner. While large corporations issue contracts routinely, the more-vested small business owner must keep the other party interested and committed throughout the process. Often, people assume the offer suggested is purely based on price and is the final offer. In my experience, large corporations rarely negotiate solely on price. Many issues negotiated by senior vice presidents or CEOs on behalf of large corporations are unrelated to pricing. It's more common for people to be flexible on some issues on the table than rigid with all the terms in their offers. Conduct research and negotiate from a position of knowledge, understanding, and openness.

Obtain Information

There are two primary levels of information you want to explore: public and private. Among the public information available are quarterly earnings calls to investors, articles written about the company in major publications, press releases, county records, published sales data, collections, balance sheets, investment portfolios, and income statements. Identifying private, privileged information may be more complicated since it may be covered by nondisclosure agreements (NDAs), or the information may be trade secrets owned by the company. Your role is to identify hidden factors and do your best to uncover them through conversations with the other party. Ask relevant questions politely and respectfully, which is how I've obtained a lot of unpublished information over the years. Public records can infer privileged information, for example, past lawsuits by vendors, employees, or consumers. It's best to do your due diligence before entering any negotiation, as it lets you leverage the information to arrive at the best deal for both parties.

Understanding BATNA

BATNA is the acronym for Best Alternative to a Negotiated Agreement. It describes the most desirable outcome a party can realistically expect to achieve if a negotiation cannot come to an agreement. Roger Fisher and William Ury introduced BATNA in their 1981 book, *Getting to Yes: Negotiating Agreement Without Giving In.* Understanding one's BATNA lets parties better assess the value of any agreement they may reach and decide whether it is worth pursuing.

If the proposed offer is better than your BATNA, you'll want to accept it. In these negotiating scenarios, BATNA sets the standard that prevents you from accepting and rejecting unfavorable terms. A good BATNA increases your negotiating power and lets you understand where to get the best possible deal. It also allows you to push harder to strengthen the proposed deal terms. To derive what your BATNA may comprise, ask yourself some of these questions in preparation:

- What is your company's reservation point and BATNA?
- How can I learn more?
- What does their BATNA say about their willingness to deal with me?
- What is the power everyone must walk away from in a situation?

Understanding the other side's needs and requirements can be a challenge. However, if you understand what the other side is thinking, you can make the best deals. Ask questions. Start a dialogue. Making your entire negotiation strategy based on assumptions without relevant facts or information is risky. Despite your chosen strategy, taking time to understand the other side's perspective can give you insights into how they will react and how certain parts of the deal might ultimately be structured.

Understand Their Authority Position
Don't assume the other negotiator has the power to agree with your proposal. Continually assess the other party's decision-making authority. Try to discover early whether the negotiator needs to speak to other parties internally before making too many compromises early on, especially when it's a complex negotiation. It's a waste of your time when, after a proposed negotiation and terms are laid out on the table, the other side states they need to chat with their boss to qualify the terms. Be aware that sometimes, authority negotiators are also known to use ambiguity about their authority as a negotiation technique. During negotiations, they seem to reach a point where you believe the discussions are over, but then they throw the authority decision to someone higher before concluding. Save yourself the grief by knowing the other side's authority position within the deal. As a strategic option, assess any potential escalation and understand whom to approach to get final approval. It will save you time and frustration during negotiations.

For example, I once flew to Tokyo for a meeting and negotiated a deal with executives with important titles in a large conference room. They were polite, professional, and prepared, and their team leader passed out a typed handout of our agenda for the meeting. In our meeting, she seemed experienced with TV retailing, my collection, and what I was trying to accomplish. She was firm about what they needed, and our meeting never got tense. After the meeting, I was confident I had accomplished what I had set out to do.

I was wrong.

After the meeting was adjourned, I followed up by email and learned that the head of the company did not like my having been only available for four visits a year. Strike one. He objected to my shows being in Tokyo and scheduled around the jewelry trade shows in Asia rather than his company's promotional advertising schedules and efforts. The head of the company objected to almost every central point we discussed during our meeting. What is the lesson? I discovered often meetings might not include the person responsible for the significant decisions. In this scenario, the meeting was used for preliminary information gathering. So I researched everything I could about the company's head and immersed myself in his vision, immediate and long-term goals, leadership methods, communication style, key motivating factors, and more. Once I had this information, we hashed out our differences, understanding who I was negotiating with. I eventually ended up with a great contract and built a healthy business in Japan due to those negotiations.

Treat Negotiation Parties as Your Partner

When negotiating, it is critical to view the other party as a collaborator or partner rather than an adversary. You and the other party may have conflicting interests, and it seems natural to think of negotiating as a zero-sum game, but remember, in *successful* negotiations there are no winners or losers. By approaching the negotiation with respect for the other party, you can reach the common goals you each intend to achieve and end up with a win win situation.

Understand What You Want

Know precisely what you want from every negotiation. List your goals in order of priority. Keep an open mind and be flexible while listening to what the other party wants from you, which may differ dramatically from what you will give up. You can navigate even the most difficult situations if you clearly understand what you need from the negotiation and what you will give up beforehand. This mindset can help foster a collaborative environment where both parties can work together to find a mutually beneficial outcome.

Remember, communication and collaboration are the essential keys to successful negotiations.

KEY TAKEAWAYS

- Negotiating is not an art or a science, but a skill honed and practiced until perfection is achieved.

- The ability to negotiate is one of the most valuable and important factors you need to take your business across the finish line.

- When negotiating, it is critical to view the other party as a collaborator or partner rather than an adversary.

- Overall, negotiations are a complex process that requires careful consideration of the needs and interests of both parties.

- Know precisely what you want from every negotiation. Then, list your goals in order of priority.

Launching Your Business

Every battle is won before it is fought.[1]

—SUN TZU

THE OPERA GAME, ALSO KNOWN AS "A NIGHT AT THE OPERA," is arguably one of the best chess games ever played. It was played in a Paris opera house in 1858 when one of the best chess players of all time, Paul Morphy, played against Duke Karl and Count Isouard. The game was so intense that some think of it as the most famous and regard it as Morphy's best game. But why is it so important? What does it have to do with launching a business? Much like the strategic game of chess, launching your business requires planning several moves in advance but being willing and prepared to adjust those moves based on your opponent's. This is how the game is won.

It is imperative to prepare for anything if you want to succeed. For example, do you remember your first job interview? What did you do? You researched information about the company, practiced your answers to potential questions, and even carefully chose your wardrobe. Why was this necessary? Because first impressions are the last impression, and in a typical job interview, opinions about a candidate are formed in the first six to ten seconds.

While I generally do not recommend forming an opinion about people so quickly, in business, first impressions are everything. That is why your launch is so important. Think of it as a series of job interviews with potential employers. Each interview could make or break your business. So, how would you prepare for the most important interview of your life? A prelaunch strategy is your opportunity to make your best first impression.

Unfortunately, many small businesses fail within the first year because their owners launch them without much preparation, hoping to fix whatever goes wrong along the way. This is the wrong approach. Nine out of ten startups will fail eventually. Only 10 percent of all new businesses will be successful in the year they launch[2] and according to a recent article in *Inc.* magazine, 45.6 percent of startups will fail within four years.[3] For example, many times I've been excited to try out a new restaurant that opened with a lot of hype, only to be disappointed with the quality of the food or service. I've also tried new nail salons that didn't meet my expectations for cleanliness, high-end gyms that were overcrowded, etc.

A solid prelaunch plan drastically increases your chances of success by laying out the steps and risks involved.

PRELAUNCH

Do not wait until after you've opened your business to start looking for customers. Creating your community before you launch gives you access to an audience that can teach you a lot along the way and help you get the product and marketing right the first time. You're pursuing your passion and dreams, and I know there is excitement, cautious hope, a dash of nervous anxiety, and most of all, unfiltered adrenaline all coursing through your body. But you must slow down and do this correctly. The most crucial task that all businesses must complete in the prelaunch phase is gather vital data, including identifying your ideal customers and their preferences, your competition, the best pricing policies, and more.

Once you have that information, you are ready to create your prelaunch marketing strategy. If executed properly, your prelaunch marketing campaign will increase awareness, create buzz, and generate leads. Using prelaunch marketing campaigns is also a terrific way to test different marketing channels as you gather feedback and data on your product. In this early stage, you can measure how your product and business are received, allowing you to fine-tune your product and marketing strategies to your defined target audience.

Your prelaunch marketing plan lets you hit the ground running with a search engine–optimized website geared toward selling in place. Use your landing page and website to generate prelaunch leads. Offer a quick and uncomplicated way to sign up for more information about your product and launch. Offer a newsletter or exclusive access to launch deals. You can track which marketing channels bring potential customers to your website once you've got them at your door by providing a straightforward way to preorder. Make sure to prominently display any reviews and influencer posts you have. Here, the key to success is providing information and added value.

You'll also want a strong online presence on social media, seeking engaged audiences ready and eager to buy, and ready to refer you to more customers. Use video teasers that don't reveal everything in your social media prelaunch marketing strategy to build anticipation. Once you have this in motion, add development updates that give insight into the product. An effective strategy I have found is to highlight team members or employees behind the scenes. Doing so builds trust with your customer and proves that your product and service work as you claim. Creating these connections with your audience can be a terrific way to make a stronger association and provide valuable storytelling opportunities supporting your brand.

Over the years, entrepreneurs have added polls and quizzes on their social sites. Participating in social media contests, challenges, and giveaways may give potential customers chances to win prizes. This is all under the umbrella of presence and influence, and it is best to have a social media presence that is active, engaging, quirky, or personal. Social media allows you to develop a relationship with your audience, building trust and credibility over time.

Finally, as part of your prelaunch plan, make sure to promote your new product with ambassadors and influencers, asking for favorable press coverage and authority. The endorsement of influencers plays a vital role in helping a new product succeed. Having a trusted influencer increases trust between people and brands. Additionally, 74 percent of consumers' purchases are informed by social media and named influencers.[4] Strong influencers can generate buzz and educate your audience about your upcoming product launch. However, choosing the right powerhouse contributors depends on your niche, product type, and budget.

You can reach out to influencers in many ways but look for active people in your space who have a similar following. The more authority or expertise they have, the better. You shouldn't limit yourself to one channel or platform since influencers are not just on social media but also blogging, podcasting, and posting on forums. It is even better to have an influencer to provide product reviews or comparisons that are great for promoting your product. Likewise, reach out to their followers and ask them for feedback.

Don't forget the press in your toolbox. Creating a press kit provides journalists and publishers with all the information they need to share your story. Your story should be easy to communicate with journalists, content writers, bloggers, podcast hosts, and influencers on social media. An effective press kit should be concise and easy to understand, and it should include the following:

- *The story of your business or brand.* Explain who you are, what you do, and the history behind your brand and business. Be sure to share any highlights in your career.

- *Biographies of your key players.* Show off the skills, qualifications, and role in the company of all your major employees. Providing this information can make the coverage you receive more personal and also tell the press who to contact for interviews.

- *Specifications.* Include a detailed fact sheet with all the information you need to discuss your product properly. Remember to note what makes your product unique and why it is superior.

- *An overview of your product or service.* Summarize the product's features and what makes it stand out from the competition.

- *Logos and branding.* Create high-quality logos and branded materials for use in any content the press creates. Ensure trademarks and registrations are in place. Protect your logo and brand name from intellectual property and trade name thieves.

- *Images of your product.* Provide high-quality images that can be easily and legally reproduced.

- *A prominent link to your press kit.* Put a prominent link to your press kit on your website or store so people can easily find it.

THE LAUNCH

Launches and openings traditionally involve in-person events or celebrations. In the digital age, hosting a virtual event can be even more accessible. This is where you would use your database of customers or email list to announce and invite potential customers to your launch. If you launch in a physical space, hosting an opening event in your new space is a good idea. Participating in a celebration, interacting with your offering, and physically touching it can profoundly affect your customer base and your relationship with them. You can use events, virtual or in-person, to

- offer limited-time offers only valid during the event to promote your products;
- engage potential customers who need a little extra push;
- stream or record the event for your social media channels;
- engage your audience in interactive learning about your product;
- generate buzz and excitement for your launch;
- engage your audience on a more personal level;
- ask and answer questions and gather great feedback; and
- have attendees share the experience and content on their personal and professional social media channels.

Events are important for gathering feedback from your target audience, whether big or small. This way, you can improve your product offering and fine-tune your approach.

AFTER THE LAUNCH

So now that your company has been launched, it's time to get moving! You'll have to make many decisions daily, and you won't get them all right. However, what matters most is that you continue to move forward. The only thing you can do is adapt on the fly.

Now is the time to develop a comprehensive marketing plan and a strategic direction toward building relationships with your customers and establishing a solid social media presence. In addition, keep up your advertising and public relations efforts after your launch. Further, tracking key performance indicators such as sales and customer feedback is essential to ensure the business is on track. Lastly, you must stay on top of industry trends and continually refine and adapt your business model and product offerings to ensure long-term success.

Long-Term Growth After the Launch

Long-term growth of your business after your launch is essential, and the specific ways to do that involve continuous investment in marketing and advertising. Focus on customer service and satisfaction as you expand your product or service offerings. Research the market and product trends and invest in research and development. Keep networking with other businesses and industry professionals to discover new niches and market opportunities as you grow your business. Analyze your data before making any business decisions to ensure you make the right choice. A wrong business decision can cause your company to fail. Utilizing customer feedback to improve your product and service offerings is one of the best ways to expand and grow your business.

Key Takeaways

- Long-term growth of your business after your launch is essential, and the specific ways to do that involve continuous investment in marketing and advertising.

- You must focus on marketing and promotion to ensure success after launching a business.

- A comprehensive press kit provides journalists and publishers with all the information they need to share your story.

- The endorsement of influencers plays a vital role in helping a new product succeed.

CHAPTER 12

Storytelling in Business

Brand storytelling is the cohesive narrative that weaves together the facts and emotions that your brand evokes.[1]
—CELINNE DA COSTA

I WAS A CURIOUS CHILD WHO GREW UP IN A SMALL VILLAGE WITH little access to entertainment, news, or current events. Our family was one of the few that owned a TV, but reception was extremely poor, and we got mostly "snow" on all three of the channels most of the time. I spent a lot of time listening to my mother tell me stories about the Korean War and how my grandmother, a widow by that time, fled her home in Seoul, on foot, with her nine children. I was horrified when I discovered what her family had gone through. I couldn't imagine what it would have been like for my grandmother to walk over two hundred miles with nine children during the frigid Korean winter. My mother was a great storyteller. The more stories she told me about her childhood, the more I became curious. I also learned to empathize, respect, admire, and love my mother and grandmother unconditionally. Such is the power of storytelling.

Storytelling is one of the oldest forms of communication. Throughout history, storytelling has played a significant role in human culture and is an essential aspect of our daily lives. For centuries, storytelling has taught us lessons, provided us with our history and sense of family, and ignited our spirit to achieve great things. Whether myths, fables, legends, or family history, storytelling appears in most societies, and it seems to be something we crave, even binge on. Research shows that the US leads the world in watching more than thirty hours of television per week, spending $90 million on movies and another $90 billion on video games.[2] As a result, stories are embedded in our consciousness, and when someone says they're going to tell a story, we are pre-programmed to expect the familiar pattern of beginning, middle, and end. In his book *Story Proof: The Science Behind the Startling Power of Story*, author Kendall Haven argues "that the steady diet of stories that children experience modifies the brain to render it more predisposed to think in story terms."[3]

ART OF EFFECTIVE STORYTELLING IN BUSINESS

The art of compelling storytelling is undeniable. But to take advantage, you must learn style and technique and develop a strong voice to succeed. The stories you tell can help you connect with your clients, prospective customers, and followers. You can build trust, communicate your mission, and manage your persona by inviting them on your journey.

Marketers in the twenty-first century follow a clear strategy based on marketing psychology. We don't have to look far to find top motivational names you might recognize, such as Richard Branson, Tim Cook, Tony Robbins, or Sheryl Sandberg, who have perfected the psychology of storytelling marketing. Three of them are well-known business leaders who appeared on *Time* magazine's list of the one hundred most influential people, but they all have one thing in common: they use stories to convey their ideas. Innovative CEO Richard Branson has been known to gather his team around a campfire to swap stories to use in the business.

Motivational speaker Tony Robbins has built an empire in and around the power of storytelling. Sharing compelling stories doesn't require you to be a high-level entrepreneur or famous CEO because, regardless of whether you are trying to sell products or services, pitch a project, close a deal, or get your team excited about one of your ideas, good stories can take you there. A compelling story helps us remember details and information. Telling a story can increase your persuasive power by creating a positive emotional state in your audience and influencing buying decisions. The ability to tell a relevant story will make you more effective in business and life. I'm sure you have experienced the power of a story when you walk out of a movie theater and dry your tears. Or perhaps after finishing a good book, you remember every word. Why? Because of the way it makes you feel. If you want to break down barriers with your audience and put your business ahead, you need to connect with them, and make an impact. People often buy on emotion and justify with logic, and very few things can do this as well as a well-told story. Deep down, we are creatures of emotion driven by feelings, fear, vanity, or security, and as a new entrepreneur, it's your job to tap into this to elicit sales.

INS AND OUTS OF BUSINESS STORYTELLING

Strong business storytelling to motivate people and build customer loyalty can be a robust content strategy. Brand awareness can be increased, and competitive advantages gained, by telling compelling stories about your company's products and services. Through business storytelling, you can motivate your team to do their best to gain a competitive advantage, encourage sales, and gain customer trust while drastically improving your brand's image, generating a long-lasting effect on the behavior and attitude of your customers, and encouraging their loyalty to your brand. Additionally, business storytelling helps leaders communicate their vision of desired beliefs and results.

Your business presentations should focus on fully understanding what you do; this is where storytelling comes into play. Stories evoke emotions, and most stories are character-driven, putting the reader in the character's shoes smack-dab in the middle of a dilemma. You need to illustrate the problem to the listener, then demonstrate how your product and services can solve it.

YOUR COMPANY MISSION STATEMENT

You, your organization, and your team need a specific mission to follow to keep your business on track. A company mission focuses on what is expected of your organization, and it should be followed whenever you make critical decisions. Technological advancements can require you to adapt and change some of your products and services, but your company mission must remain the same. For example, the mission statement for Victoria Wieck Jewelry, "To create uniquely designed fine jewelry for the modern woman, never compromising quality or style," helped clarify and simplify some of the most critical decisions we faced. I can't count how many times a major retail store buyer requested prices that would have required reducing our product quality, sometimes by a little bit, other times by a lot. In a few cases, I've even sold a few styles at a much lower profit margin than we needed to balance out a collection for a good customer, but we never did it in exchange for reducing quality or offering outdated styles. I believe this commitment to my original mission helped in many ways, including in building solid, trusting relationships with my suppliers, employees, and most importantly, the consumers who buy and wear my jewelry.

BRANDING

Branding is about building a reputation with the customer, and it should always follow your company's mission statement. One of the most effective ways to build a brand is to create a succinct, yet compelling, brand story about how some of your core products were developed and how they help people. Your brand story should include what values you share with your customers and how it aligns with the specific function, design, and quality of your products. With their permission, you can share interesting stories of how your customers' lives were elevated or changed by using your products. Your brand story should align with all your communications with your customers or potential customers, including your website, email blasts, and advertising.

THE IMPORTANCE OF EMOTIONS IN BUYING DECISIONS

Despite millions of years of evolution, humans still rely heavily on emotions in making decisions. Regardless of your data analysis and research, consumer decision-making is more likely to be influenced by primal brain functions. Marketers, understanding the science, must therefore be masters of connecting emotionally with customers and clients.

Douglas Van Praet, author of *Unconscious Branding: How Neuroscience Can Empower (and Inspire) Marketing*, states, "The most startling truth is we don't even think our way to logical solutions. We feel our way to reason. Emotions are the substrate, the base layer of neural circuitry underpinning even rational deliberation. Emotions don't hinder decisions. On the contrary, they constitute the foundation on which they're made!"[4] I couldn't agree more. In my experience with customers around the world, I have found that most purchases are emotional. How else can you explain successfully selling jewelry during some of the most devastating economic times? For example, during the 2008 financial meltdown and the COVID-19 pandemic, surely, jewelry would be considered one of the least necessary products for human survival during such extremely challenging economic times, yet customers continued to buy it.

An emotional purchase is influenced by feelings rather than rational considerations. Consumer behavior and decision-making processes are explored through this area of research. We know that emotions have a significant impact on consumer choices. When individuals evaluate products or brands, both emotional and analytical systems are involved: customers process emotions and memories and also evaluate information logically, weighing the pros and cons.

Personal and emotionally compelling stories help build an emotional connection with your target audience. Consider the phrase, "People will forget what you said, people will forget what you did, but people will never forget how you made them feel." Customers will have a personal stake in your brand when you create an emotional connection with them.

I've observed, in my thirty-five years of business, that brands that share customers' values garner significantly more loyalty from them. Stories can bring your company's human side to life, highlighting the people behind the business, including yourself. You can use your life experiences as a springboard, showing how you overcame specific challenges, how your work is making a difference in the lives of those around you. All this builds trust and loyalty with your audience, creating a sense of community and connection.

Stories are also a powerful tool to help your audience understand the complex information related to your business. You can use stories to explain abstract concepts, provide context, and make information more relatable regarding the products you are offering. You can also use stories to demonstrate your company's value, showcase customer success stories, and illustrate the impact of your products and services across your given industry, making the information easier to comprehend for your audience.

MECHANICS OF STORYTELLING FOR YOUR BUSINESS

Now that we have identified the key concepts and discussed the science behind the story, let's look at the mechanics of implementing storytelling for your business, crafting a compelling story, and applying it. Remember, the story doesn't have to be your own, you can often find stories all around you that are relatable to your product and service.

Authentic Stories Make an Impact

Wherever your story comes from, be sure it is authentic. There is something attractive about authenticity. Eighty percent of consumers say they are compelled to engage with a company when it provides authentic content.[5] Unfortunately, finding what's real in a world filled with misinformation, fake news, and alternative facts is more difficult today than ever, so do your due diligence.

So, how do you come up with unique, authentic stories? You can use reviews from your customers, success stories from employees, an overview of how and why you developed the company's mission statement, maybe team challenges you've overcome.

Remember, storytelling differs from presenting a message, but your story must support your message and impact the listener's emotions.

Crafting Your Story

How many times have you shared a joke without making anyone crack a smile? We've all experienced it, our retelling gone flat. That's because it's not just about identifying what you want to say, it's also about how you say it and, most of all, how you deliver it. This is why comedians practice their pitch, story, and joke delivery to the extreme, all to relate to their audience. The same applies to you and your business. Ensure you craft your story so your audience will relate to it.

To keep your audience engaged, you'll need a well-constructed narrative to draw them in. A story with a confusing timeline, references your audience doesn't understand, or pacing that's too fast or too slow will fail. Keep the structure of your story straightforward, but make it vivid with detailed imagery and characters, always having a conflict or struggle. Take the classic "hero's journey" route: a protagonist embarks on a quest, faces challenges, and then succeeds.

Draw your listener in by describing a scene using strong and captivating details. Then describe the event and what is happening at that moment vividly and candidly. Introduce the struggle or the problem to create conflict and trigger emotions. Keep your story concise and easy to share to encourage retelling.

An Easy-to-Follow Story Structure

The three steps of good storytelling are often called the story arc or narrative arc. Storytelling generally begins with a hook (which engages the audience), moves into a middle section (where a dramatic twist usually occurs), and ends with a conclusion (which resolves problems or inspires action).

Hooks can either be problems or journeys that need to be solved. A hook is meant to pique the reader's curiosity and create empathy for the protagonist.

More information is then provided about the character's challenges or conflicts in the middle of the story. Emotionally, this story element highlights how adversity impacts the characters and the changes they must undergo before a resolution can be found.

As the main character overcomes their problems, the story leads to an inspiring and informative ending, at which point you can explain to your audience how it relates to your product and/or service.

Telling a great story is about helping others understand unfamiliar concepts and ideas and ultimately persuading them to take action. You need to connect with your audience by knowing their pain points and using your knowledge of your product and yourself. What will motivate your clients to make a purchase? Ultimately, it's about how your product, idea, or concept relieves their pain or increases their pleasure. Be sure to end your pitch in an action-oriented and emotional way so your audience knows what to do next.

The Real Hero Is Your Audience

You can't be your story's hero. We all know people who love to brag about themselves and their achievements—and we also know how boring these stories can be. Audiences won't respond to speakers who portray themselves as saviors. You shouldn't be the central character who saves the day, but you can provide the tools (your product) to the main character so they can solve the problem and save the day. Instead of saying, "This is what my product does," try saying, "This is what you can do with my product, idea, or solution." People should see themselves in your story if you want them to adopt your ideas. And here, the more specific, the better because, at this stage, you want to strike a chord with your audience. Add all pertinent details; present relatable characters, scenarios, and situations; activate your audience's senses; and make them feel the power of your narration to make your story come to life.

Visuals and Video Storytelling

Initially, I had no idea what I was doing when I began retailing on TV. However, I have spent the last twenty plus years telling powerful, inspirational, compelling stories on live TV in front of millions of people. I gave you a brief description of my TV background for quite a simple reason—I believe the entire world will move to video. As a result, there is a video mechanism in every platform's user interface. Facebook, Instagram, Pinterest, YouTube, and even LinkedIn have incorporated some live-streaming components. Why? Because it works.

As a writer and author, I continued to hear the old saying, "Show, don't tell." Not only is video an effective way to show large numbers of people what your product or service can do, but it also increases the likelihood that your story will be remembered. Research shows that information retained from one minute of online video equals 1.8 million words.[6] That is power.

It is easier to recall a story than a list of facts or promises, and it is even more memorable when combined with video imagery. Creating a visual story will keep your company at the forefront of your customers' minds despite competition. Additionally, with the power of using video storytelling, you can build an amazing, memorable, premium brand without spending a lot of money. Now, I'm not saying it will be free. Don't be afraid to spend a little money to create a quality product. Once you master the art of storytelling, combine it with high-quality video content to tell compelling stories dramatized with facts, and your company and brand could potentially skyrocket.

Video imagery that uses animation, overlays, text, and more to engage your viewers is essential. You can use your newly produced video on social media platforms, send it out via email, newsletters, and your website to engage your users directly. Remember not to overdo it. Use only information that adds to your story to avoid overwhelming your message.

What Should You Do First?

Now you know how valuable video and storytelling are to your brand. What do you need to get started? Before anything, make sure your story makes sense on paper. For success, make sure your process is clear and focused. If it's not, it probably won't make sense on camera.

Never forget who your target market and audience are when making your video. Often, the production of the video, along with any technical issues you may experience, can make you veer off course, producing something that doesn't hit the mark. As we discussed, the first step in a marketing campaign is to develop a marketing plan and define the target audience. Time spent understanding who your viewers are, their interests, and any problems they may face as you create your video is time well spent. Using this information, you can build your narrative around the "pain points" of your audience. As a result, they will watch your videos closely, hoping your story will teach them how to solve their problems or change their perspective. Develop your story around achieving these creative narrative arcs. There are two essential types of storyboards for business storytelling videos: factual and fictional.

Factual Storyboard

A factual video storyboard is precisely what it sounds like. It is an accurate visual representation of the narrative and flows that you envision for your video. Use this storyboard to plan and visualize your video before it is shot. This will assist you and everyone involved in identifying any potential problems or areas for improvement for maximum impact. Your factual video storyboard should include sketches or drawings, images of your product, live characters, or animations that illustrate the main points you want to make. In addition, the storyboard sketch should include a brief description of each scene and list any audio or visual elements used.

Fictional Storyboard

A fictional storyboard can be developed by brainstorming ideas, considering the purpose of your video, your target audience, and the overall message you want to communicate in your makeshift script. Once you have your basic concept for your video description, include a detailed description of the action dialogue and any other elements that will be included in the video. Here is a framework for your fictional and factual story, which you can use as a starting point:

- Choose a protagonist (you or someone else) who aligns with your target audience's goals.
- Pinpoint your customers' problem and pain point.

- Describe the quest or journey that brought you to your product or service.

- Arrive at the solution and resolution that your product or service brings.

You can enhance your video story by following these additional strategies and tips:

- *Relate to your audience.* More people will relate to your story if it shares a common human experience.

- *Take an economic approach.* The video should be structured so that each part drives the story forward.

- *Consider the point of view.* You should write a story from the perspective of a typical target audience member. Consider their perspective rather than the company's.

- *Keep your tone natural and informal.* By doing so, you'll be able to connect with audiences and help them understand your message.

- *Consider the design and visual factors.* Lights, costuming, and color palette are among these. Your video storytelling message and goals will be better supported if these are done well.

The essential and ever-present reality of business and video storytelling draws people in, their attention spans are held, and they feel invested in the story. Video storytelling requires time and effort, but success can pay off in thousands of views, increased brand recognition, and other benefits. If you have a modest budget, it's worth investigating the visual storytelling options and how to use them to improve your brand and customer engagement.

KEY TAKEAWAYS

- Stories are a powerful tool for helping your audience understand the complex information related to your business.

- Modern stories follow a similar progression, regardless of genre or purpose. In storytelling, this progression is known as the narrative arc.

- Video storytelling has the power to provide valuable information, and by telling a memorable story, you can educate your customers.

- A fictional storyboard can be developed by brainstorming ideas, considering the purpose of your video, your target audience, and the overall message you want to communicate.

- A factual video storyboard is an accurate visual representation of the narrative and flows that you envision for your video.

CHAPTER 13

Managing Growing Pains

Learn from every mistake because every experience, encounter and particularly mistakes are there to teach you and force you into being more of who you are.[1]

—OPRAH WINFREY

WHEN MY DAUGHTER WAS YOUNG, I PLAYED CHESS WITH HER. AT first, I let her win, letting her think she was smarter. I used chess to help her develop, mature, and learn the life lesson of winning and losing. I was never good at chess and didn't want to spend hours practicing, but I knew enough about the game to know it would be good for her to learn valuable lessons about life. As she learned the game, it didn't take her long to start winning. The game of chess, much like growing a business, is won both on the board and in the mind. Once this concept is understood, practiced, and executed well, it will give you the winning advantage.

Growing your business requires strategic planning, taking calculated risks, and, most importantly, adapting to changing conditions. Successful growth and survival in the long term requires thinking about the game and its strategy before playing. Every business, large or small, experiences growing pains, and much like chess, you must recognize the obstacles in the way of making the right moves for your business and create strategies to circumvent them. Unfortunately, while busy managing the hectic aspects of their business, most young entrepreneurs make these moves haphazardly, leading to many business failures. Much like understanding your opponent's chess moves and options, knowing the exact obstacles you might face is the first step in figuring out how to avoid them. As you grow, you must develop a lens or framework with related tools to help you successfully understand and manage your new business's growth.

MANAGING GROWING PAINS

"Growing pains" is a term commonly used by CEOs to explain a wide range of issues experienced by expanding businesses. No matter how you describe them, growing pains are real, and you must recognize them as necessary challenges to overcome in order to reach the next level. Some challenges you will likely face include

- hiring experienced staff;
- offering competitive employee benefits;
- maintaining company culture and a high level of customer service;
- overworked and overwhelmed employees;
- a shortage of funds to finance new orders;
- acquiring or leasing larger spaces for office space, warehouse, or shipping facilities quickly;
- maintaining high quality control standards;
- maxing out manufacturing capacities;
- shipment delays;
- increased competition; and
- decreasing profit margins.

As you grow your business and encounter these (and potentially other, unforeseen) challenges and difficulties, you must develop a lens or framework with tools to help you understand and successfully manage them.

The most important thing is to ensure that the steps you take today build a solid framework for achieving aggressive yet sustainable growth in the future. Here are some of the most common challenges small business owners face as they attempt to grow their businesses at an aggressive rate:

- Maintaining market relevance
- Preparing for the future
- Managing cash flow and finances
- Identifying and solving problems
- Systematizing
- Managing personality traits and skills

Maintaining Market Relevance

Researching the market before launching your business is not something you do only once. Business conditions constantly change, so consistently performing market research is a necessity. You must be current on market trends, relevant technological advancements, changes in consumer behavior, and changes your competitors make. Making important decisions using out-of-date information often leads to failure. The hard truth is that success brings attention, and one pain of growing your business is competitors taking notice. You must know what they are doing because the more successful you are, the more your competitors will notice you—and react to your success. By leveraging what they learn from you and offering better deals, your competitors can lure away your customers who choose their product offerings over yours. Because of mishaps and trial by fire, I've learned that over time, products and services age, sales growth slows, and profit margins shrink. Your products and customer service must evolve continuously to grow your revenue and profits. Identifying where your products are in their life cycles and finding ways to extend that life cycle can help maximize profitability. Identify potential trends and upswings in your current market conditions using your own research data and published information. Develop an in-depth understanding of what your customers want, how they behave, and which marketing approaches work best for them. As Starbucks did with its customer feedback campaign, talking to your customers and evaluating their feedback will give you real-world insight for the future.

Preparing for the Future

What made sense a year ago might not work today. As market conditions change, you must revisit and update your business goals and implement new strategies to adapt to changing circumstances. In order to grow your business aggressively, you must attract a healthy percentage of new customers to counterbalance the natural attrition rate for your business. For instance, if you own a weight loss center, you should expect to lose a significant percentage of customers every month as they start to lose their excess weight. Regular customers may relocate away from your business or their financial situations may change, causing their buying preferences to shift. Setting up a framework for generating new customers is vital. I've always tried attracting at least 15 percent more new customers annually. One way to do this is to set up a referral reward system and affiliate programs with other businesses in your area.

To achieve aggressive growth, you also need to create an environment for your existing customers to buy more frequently and trust you enough to buy higher-priced products with value-added types of packaging, product extensions, and expanded product lines. Strategically implemented plans to reward and solidify existing business relationships will provide reliable cash flow and greater profit potential. Similar to a new business launch, every significant move requires planning and action. Be careful of being too opportunistic. There is a fine line, so you must question and examine if your latest ideas suit your company's strengths and vision, along with supporting where the business is going, and if it's not a fit—don't do it. Bear in mind that every new development brings with it changing risks. It's worth regularly reviewing the risks you face and developing contingency plans.

Managing Cash Flow and Finances

Good cash flow is crucial for a growing business, as cash constraints can be one of the biggest factors limiting your growth. Business planning and assessing new opportunities should include using your finances best. Unfortunately, eager entrepreneurs are prone to making costly mistakes—products that don't sell, advertising campaigns that fail to deliver, and customers who fail to pay on time or do not pay at all. One of the most important skills I've learned is limited market testing, which I do before launching a product to my target market. And even though I've had the good fortune to generate hundreds of millions of dollars in sales, I still test all my styles before investing money in expensive product development or marketing costs associated with new product launches. If someone you trusted could provide you with accurate information so that every product you offer would sell out at the price you charge, what would that information be worth to you? The answer: it would be priceless. If you master the art of lost-cost testing, you can obtain valuable information in real time. Here are some of the most impactful ways I've managed my cash flow.

Purchasing Accounts Receivable Insurance

Even though I sold to various internationally recognized retail chains, I always carried accounts receivable insurance, which paid off in more ways than one. First, securing accounts receivable insurance for all my corporate customers gave me peace of mind. As we all know, even some of the largest companies can file for bankruptcy with little or no notice, and knowing I would get paid no matter what they did on all outstanding purchase orders was a game-changer for me. Second, your financial risk on all the customers you insure goes down to zero. Third, you get to find out the financial health of potential customers before you do any business with them, saving you time and money. Fourth, anytime you want to sell to a large account, you can contact your accounts receivable agent and ask them if they would insure them before you or anyone from your team make the initial call. Finally, do you remember the massive consolidation that took place back in the 1990s? At that time, several of my high-end department store customers couldn't pay and went bankrupt, but I still got paid by my insurance company.

Establishing a Discount System for Early Payment

Generally, the larger the account, the slower the payment, which can tie up precious cash flow when you need it the most. Consider offering a discount for paying early. For small- to medium-sized wholesalers, you can provide a significant discount for paying immediately, such as cash on delivery (COD). Even for large corporate customers that operate on net 90- to net 120-day terms, by offering some discount, you can shorten their payment terms to net 30.

Factoring

"Factoring" in business means obtaining immediate funds, typically between 70 to 90 percent on the future income associated with a business invoice. The actual percentage your bank would factor depends on the bank, your company's creditworthiness, and your customer's credit history with their vendors. The most important fact to remember is that factoring allows a small business to have access to a substantial portion of their outstanding invoices for a small fee by pledging their invoices for collateral. Managing working capital efficiently is a major hurdle and a growing pain for any business. By exploring the various options, you could find ways to improve your cash flow without accepting additional risk.

IDENTIFYING AND SOLVING PROBLEMS

In my business circles I've seen many new businesses operating in perpetual crisis mode. This is not healthy and can lead to company failure and demise. Putting out fires at every turn is exhausting and not sustainable. Even though short-term crises are always urgent, they may not matter as much as other things you could do in the larger picture. For example, a lack of intellectual property protection could cause your business to be increasingly at risk. Or perhaps you're focusing on individual marketing campaigns when your brand needs more development resources. What would you do if one of your primary manufacturer's factories shut down due to a massive fire? That scenario happened to me years ago. It was highly stressful then, but I learned much from that experience. Since then, I've learned to not depend on only one factory, even for a highly specialized category. Instead, I diversify my manufacturing circle. Whatever the case, to avoid constantly being in a state of emergency, you need to stay ahead of problems and prioritize your attention to identify what is causing conflict and stagnation and what is driving growth.

Systematizing

Most new businesses produce and rely on data, including customer interactions, employee training, financial records, strategic pricing, and regulatory requirements. Without suitable systems, the data from these parts of doing business is often too much to keep track of, let alone use effectively. You must learn to delegate responsibilities and tasks as your business grows. I am not suggesting you delegate everything. Instead, I recommend setting parameters when you begin to assign tasks to others. Yes, your employees will make mistakes, but they will learn valuable lessons from those mistakes. Again, it's essential to set clear boundaries so that the mistakes your employees can make are limited. You cannot manage effectively without accurate information systems and communication between your team members and you. Information sharing and coordinating different functions becomes more challenging as your business grows, and a key component in avoiding this dominant growing pain is putting the proper infrastructure in place. Investing in the right systems pays off in the short and long term.

Managing Personality Traits and Skills

Individuals are responsible for creating and growing businesses worldwide. However, these same individuals have traits that can be accountable for holding them back. To grow your business, you must learn to delegate correctly, trust your team, and refrain from micromanaging every detail on a day-to-day basis. You must develop your time management skills to keep on top of everything, focus on what's important, and listen to others' advice as the business becomes more complex.

Embracing Change

Complacency is one of the significant obstacles and growing pains for any business. It is a major threat to your growing business. Even megacorporations can become obsolete due to complacency. I recommend regularly reevaluating and updating your business objectives to stay competitive in changing market conditions.

Make sure members of your supply chain keep up with the changes in the overall marketplace as well. You need suppliers who can meet your needs as your business grows and adapts to change. Consistency and reliability may be more important as your business grows than finding the lowest prices. For example, you want to review any contracts you have periodically to accommodate increased volume and other changes, developing new training methods and elevate your customer service, and maintaining a technological edge.

Even if it takes you outside your comfort zone, you must fully commit to your strategy. And along the way, there may be complex decisions, and if you aren't prepared to make them, your business may suffer a severe competitive disadvantage. As we grow, our bodies undergo many, often confusing, growing pains, but they paved the way to adulthood. In other words, growing pains are necessary for eventual growth. The sooner you embrace change with enthusiasm and optimism, the sooner you will master the skills you need to scale your business to the next level.

KEY TAKEAWAYS

- Entrepreneurship is difficult, and a large percentage of small businesses fail for numerous reasons, including lack of visibility, funds, and unsustainable profit margins.

- "Growing pains" is a term commonly used by CEOs to explain a wide range of shortcomings.

- Every business, large or small, experiences growing pains, and much like in the game of chess, you must know the moves and, most importantly, what is standing in your way of making those moves.

- Researching the market before launching your business isn't something you do once.

- Business conditions change constantly, so consistently perform market research.

- Most new businesses produce and rely on information, including customer interactions, employee details, financial records, strategic pricing, and regulatory requirements.

CHAPTER 14

How to Avoid GROWING Broke

Like a fire that burns too fast, a business that grows too quickly without sufficient resources to finance its hypergrowth can become extinct.

—Victoria Wieck

Isn't it every entrepreneur's dream to sell their products to as many people as possible? The fastest way to achieve exponential growth is to attract a few large retailers to increase visibility, revenue, and profits. But we've all heard the adage, "Be careful what you wish for." I cannot count how many entrepreneurs put their heart and soul into their business, endure years of long hours, and finally reach their pinnacle, only to go bankrupt and end up with nothing.

If worked at hard enough, nearly every business will generate a profit and sustain long-term growth. The problem most entrepreneurs experience is that after reaching a desired level of success, they take their eyes off the prize and become complacent. They operate haphazardly and miss pertinent details, and then, they *grow* bankrupt. How often have you heard a business owner tout, "My business is growing by leaps and bounds, and my sales are great! I don't understand why I don't have any cash?" As you grow your business, your margins get tighter, but if you don't understand this bigger picture, your business can and will grow broke.

Growing pains are typical in every business, and you probably are not doing the right things if you aren't experiencing them. And going broke has everything to do with not attracting enough business and not making enough money to cover expenses and payroll.

Growing broke, however, is entirely different. Growing too fast without a foundational grip can cause everything to teeter, causing your seemingly successful business to hang in the balance. For example, if you sell food to several mom-and-pop restaurants and stores, your margins should be reasonably good. But when faced with selling to giant corporations, such as HSN, Walmart, Whole Foods, and other retailers, your margins will decrease. If you allow this to continue, you will finally reach a point where your business will ultimately fail.

Based on my experience working with hundreds of entrepreneurs across the country from numerous industries, I believe businesses risk failure if they try to grow too quickly without simple processes and systems firmly in place. Perhaps the strangest example of this was the children's modeling clay Play-Doh. The product was initially sold as a cleaner for removing coal residue from wallpaper. Then, in the 1950s, demand for the clay plummeted as oil and gas furnaces became more popular, and the makers considered shutting down the business—until luck intervened. The company's owners heard about schoolteachers in Cincinnati, Ohio, using Play-Doh clay in arts and crafts classes, and the children loved it. Recognizing the vast potential of marketing the product as a children's toy, the company pivoted, and it became the craft item everyone loved. Now owned by Hasbro, Play-Doh has sold over two billion cans around the globe. This is an example of a company, once excelling in one market, quickly pivoting to stay relevant and avoid bankruptcy.

The belief that achieving $1 million in gross profits indicates success is common among small business owners. Despite high gross profit figures, many owners struggle to make their businesses profitable. An organization with ten employees might pay $700,000 in payroll and payroll-related expenses, such as employee benefits, leaving $300,000 for operations owner's compensation. An owner might easily earn less than their employees if you include costs such as office rent; health insurance; marketing expenses; debt accrual payments; local, state, and federal taxes; and ongoing technology expenses. A young or small business can run reasonably well without much planning by just addressing new projects or challenges as they arise. The business's short-term goals dictate this. Every mistake becomes more costly as your business grows. If you sell to several thousand customers, a $2 pricing mistake will cost you $4,000 ($2 per unit x 2,000 customers). However, if your business sold 100,000 units to large retailers, a $2 pricing error could cost you $200,000. Consider that large retailers require heavy discounts in the first place, and a $200,000 loss in income could be devastating. Your risk of growing broke increases substantially, and any weakness in your business will amplify and seep into various areas of your business. Uncontrolled, hyperfast growth can be hazardous.

In my world, I have witnessed far too many new entrepreneurs build seemingly successful businesses and reach a certain level, only to make the huge mistake of not keeping their eye on the finish line, and ultimately go out of business. For example, several jewelry manufacturers have grown their businesses over the years, only to go bankrupt after decades of steady growth. Susan M. is a third-generation jeweler passionate about taking her family's jewelry business to the next level. As the Internet and online shopping grew, she struggled to keep the doors open at her store. She knew she had to do everything she could to expand her business, so Susan spent thousands of dollars building an e-commerce website and started a blog to help drive traffic to her site. Next, she hired a social media expert, made relevant business relationships with top-tier manufacturers, networked with local businesses, and joined several national professional organizations. After years of attending trade shows and contacting retailers, she finally got the break she sought.

A major TV network's jewelry buyer was interested in some of her designs. She jumped on the opportunity immediately. Her first purchase order from this TV network was for a 14K gold necklace, totaling over $180,000, approximately a 35 percent gross profit margin, significantly lower than her store's average gross margin. The TV retailer explained that the $180,000 order was a small test order and that there could be much larger orders along the way if all went well with their test order. The order was for 2,500 necklaces at $72 each. Susan's cost of goods was $46.80 each. She was still excited to obtain a purchase order from a prestigious TV retailer and receive a $63,000 gross profit.

Next, Susan hired Alice to take over the management, buying, and store operations so she could focus on growing her TV retailing and other significant ways of increasing her distribution. The buyer from the TV station told her that her necklace sold out very quickly and that they wanted to place a much larger order and give it more airtime than the last time. They wanted to order 10,000 necklaces, but at $54 each. They explained that to sell 10,000 units, they would need to offer a much lower price. This request put Susan between a rock and a hard place because she was about to take a $540,000 risk, and the best she could hope for was a $72,000 gross profit. She tried her best to negotiate a better price but wasn't successful. Finally, she convinced herself there would be plenty of opportunities to make much better profits and took the order. Over the next few months, Susan spent a small fortune meeting with manufacturers worldwide to develop new products for TV retailers.

However, during her next meeting with the buyer at the TV station, she was told that her necklace didn't sell as well as they had hoped and that they needed to return 4,000 units for a full credit before placing another order. They had already generated a chargeback of $216,000 against Susan's vendor number. This chargeback was more than Susan's total profits from the TV retailer. Susan made $135,000 in gross profit earnings between both orders and would lose $81,000 after all her efforts. She would need to pay freight and arrange for the return of the 4,000 necklaces. It would take years to sell 4,000 units at her store. Susan's actual loss was much more significant than what the numbers in this equation suggest because she had to hire extra personnel to operate her store, incur packaging and shipping costs to ship her orders, hire outside contractors to meet the TV retailer's quality control requirements, obtain the required product liability insurance, and pay product development and travel costs.

Susan was lucky to be in the jewelry business because her products do not face expiration dates and could be melted down for raw materials to recover some of her costs. Unfortunately, in specific categories such as cosmetics, hair care, or food, products are stamped with expiration dates and lose their value daily. I've known vendors who resorted to paying to destroy their products instead of paying warehousing costs. Susan was on her way to growing broke but still hoped to make it big in the TV retail arena. She accepted the $216,000 return and got her buyer to generate a much larger order. Unfortunately, it didn't take long before she went bankrupt.

I've watched so many friends start and work very hard to grow businesses only to grow broke. Uncontrolled growth or growing your business too fast can be dangerous. I understand where you are. You have worked diligently, watching your business scale and grow after carefully developing a viable product around which you can build a business that is your passion. In a short period, you've seen excellent results—sales are up, customers are enthusiastic, and the market appears to be growing. In your mind, growing now is the ideal and perfect time to do it fast. Yet, before diving in headfirst, you must stop and fully assess the situation. Growing a business too quickly can be just as unsuccessful as not growing it at all. But what are the dangers of rapid growth, and how do you avoid them?

KEEP DIVERSIFYING, DIVERSIFYING, AND DIVERSIFYING

I learned from business school that you should always diversify. You should never have any one customer account for more than 10 percent of your business. In the early years of my entrepreneurship, I used to think my professors had been too theoretical and that I would be better off if I had only three or four customers to deal with. Over the years, I've come close to losing everything because one or more of my customers either couldn't pay on time or wanted to pay lower prices than my costs. I eventually decided that the only way I could grow comfortably was to diversify my customer and manufacturing bases simultaneously.

Additionally, I added diversity to my product range to achieve growth. When HSN approached me, I was already a reliable vendor for many department stores, duty-free stores, cruise ship gift shops, and small wholesalers worldwide. As I obtained millions of dollars in orders, instead of focusing solely on existing customers, I needed to find new customers as quickly as possible so that my orders from HSN didn't represent more than 10 percent of my total revenue stream. In addition, I expanded my business geographically so that if there was a recession in one part of the world, my business in other regions would still be stable. Over the years, when a buyer from any company asked me for "marketing support" to discount my products or chargebacks of any kind, I navigated those negotiations to benefit both parties. Diversifying your manufacturing or vendor base is vital to securing your growth. During the hypergrowth phase of my business, being able to count on several eager and capable suppliers who wanted to grow with me was a key factor in my success.

KEEP FINANCES UNDER CONTROL

Excessive growth is caused by your business outpacing your ability to comprehend its size and scale. In most instances, when your business is small, you probably know your numbers pretty well. You can easily keep track of your cash flow and see how expenses compare to sales. However, when you reach a specific sales range, say $5 million or more, keeping track of your finances becomes exceptionally challenging on a large scale. Investing a little money to grow is understandable, but you must weigh risk versus reward carefully before spending large amounts of capital. Budgeting and understanding your cash flow is essential, along with having systems and operations firmly in place. Stay on top of examining data on your company, keeping the broad scope in mind. Besides looking at all your company's data, evaluate data from other companies like yours to help you understand the context of your decisions to avoid business failure.

AVOID MISTAKES IN CASH FLOW

In nearly every failed business, you are likely to find mistakes made in cash flow. In business, there is no doubt that cash flow mistakes are prevalent, and they are a significant reason why many small businesses fail. An overly optimistic growth projection or failure to understand the difference between profit and actual cash on hand can spell disaster for your business. For example, many entrepreneurs don't understand that the inventory on their books for full value for years and years is worth very little. They might be better off liquidating it at a reasonable price and generating cash flow to put the proceeds to productive use. You can easily reach a point where your monthly expenses exceed your operating capital as your business grows. Of course, you won't be sunk if you plan ahead, but if you're not careful, you could be one bad month away from sinking if you don't keep the money coming in.

DON'T OVERVALUE SALES

Some entrepreneurs believe everything else will follow if they take care of sales. However, those numbers don't tell the whole story. You should use all your information when making financial decisions: revenue is a valuable metric, but so are the various costs necessary to generate sales. Deciding to grow your business should be based on a solid financial evaluation, including market studies, economic analyses, and any other available data. Growing well is much more complex than simply growing.

OPERATE AS EFFICIENTLY AS POSSIBLE

The more you grow, the more you need to be organized. First, you must develop a system for everyone in your company to follow. Fast and loose may have worked for your small team but not so much for a larger group. It becomes increasingly important to stay organized as your ranks grow and positions that used to be filled by individuals become teams of people. Access to information is vital: cost estimates, budgets, cash flow, sales, and inventory. Working together as a team around the core principles that have made your company successful is crucial, and getting organized is critical.

A great startup happens because you can create balance within your small team of great people. However, hiring people who check all the boxes and can perform various tasks as needs arise becomes more difficult as your business grows. In addition, when you're in growth mode, your business requires people with specific skills, often requiring an adjustment in company culture and processes.

As your business grows, you must step back periodically and see the bigger picture. Unfortunately, most founders become engrossed in the minute day-to-day details and lose focus on the overall mission. While you should not micromanage, you should also be careful not to become detached from your business's daily realities. Successful entrepreneurs learn to let their employees make small mistakes in a controlled environment to let them grow as individuals as well as valuable employees for the future of their company.

THE TIME IS NOW

While it's exciting to grow your business, managing growth is essential. As you've seen in this chapter, growth for your company can be dangerous without the right approach. You should build your business to scale so business operations, technology, customer service, and human resources grow at the same pace.

Growing fast is positive, but the fast-forward movement can lead to failure. Most entrepreneurs don't realize they are growing broke until it's too late. Do everything within your power to avoid growing past your limitations and growing broke.

Before you even begin growing, it is smart to create a clear map of how you'll expand. Make sure you're following your map by monitoring your progress and setting alarms to alert you if things go off track. Tracking progress and anticipating problems is essential, but don't let performance targets hinder creativity and innovation.

Businesses constantly evolve, so you must be committed to continuous improvement to scale up and exit without growing broke. Unfortunately, it is easy to get stuck in a "we've always done it this way" mentality that limits learning and growth.

We all want to grow our business and increase profit and revenue. In creating a sustainable million-dollar business, the key to avoiding growing broke is to remain vigilant in all operations and organizational systems and diversify your customer base. Manage your cash flow, examining the market and trends, including pricing and margins, to ensure your business grows with equilibrium and is not one-sided, which can leave your business falling short and growing broke. Understanding your numbers and every facet of the business, as well as not being complacent and remaining diligent, is the foundation for all your successful business growth and, ultimately, not growing broke.

KEY TAKEAWAYS

- Manage your cash flow, examining the market and trends, including pricing and margins, to ensure your business grows with equilibrium and is not one-sided.

- Make sure you're on track by monitoring your progress and setting alarms.

- Growing pains are typical in every business, and you probably are not doing the right things if you aren't experiencing them.

- Going broke has everything to do with not attracting enough business and not making enough money to cover expenses and payrolls.

- Growing broke is growing too fast without a foundational grip.

Scaling Your Business

*Good business leaders create a vision, articulate it, passion-
ately own it, and relentlessly drive it to completion.*[1]

—JACK WELCH

I HAVE SPENT MANY YEARS PURSUING MY BUSINESS DREAMS.
Along the journey, I witnessed my business growing, yet after
countless trials, errors, and failings, I discovered the massive difference and correlation between growing and scaling a business.

Growing your business means increasing sales and revenue,
adding new customers, and increasing expenses. In a typical
business, growth is *only* achieved by adding more expenses and
resources, such as additional capital and employees. Most businesses will reach a point of diminishing returns as they invest
more money and other resources into their businesses.

Scaling your business means growing your business at a much
faster rate without spending proportionally more money. As your
business scales, you discover necessary changes to your operation
that must be addressed or your system will break, leaving expenses
to rise uncontrollably. Unfortunately, many business owners are
unaware of these problems until it is too late, and I want to change
this for you.

How a business scales is different in a small business, a startup, and a profitable company. Most Fortune 500 companies began as mere business ideas but were scaled by passionate entrepreneurs. So what are the details involved in scaling for a small business? It takes a strategic plan and flawless execution to prepare your business for scaling. As a strategy to scale, I have found the following to be effective:

- Focusing on your core business
- Systemizing
- Innovating
- Elevating and enhancing
- Dominating your industry

FOCUSING ON YOUR CORE BUSINESS

To scale, you need to strengthen your core business, the part of your business where you have a competitive advantage. You have probably heard the saying, "You can't please everyone." This could not be more true. Whenever a potential supplier tells me they are the best source for diamonds, pearls, gold chains, and emeralds, I politely thank them and end our conversation as quickly as possible. Why? Because I know better and understand that it takes enormous expertise in pearls and a small fortune to own a pearl farm that requires government licenses in Japan, China, or the Philippines to lease a part of the ocean and grow them over several years. This fact alone makes it impossible for the same supplier to be the prime source for diamond mining in Africa simultaneously. Focus on your core strengths and use your expertise to build dominance in the marketplace. Scaling may require reducing your product offerings rather than expanding.

Since I believed a wide selection was necessary to attract high-volume customers, I resisted having to delete some of my favorite styles. I was wrong. I needed to be laser-focused on my strengths and offer only a few of my better selling styles, giving myself a clear competitive advantage to scale. As a result, my product offerings went from hundreds of styles to just under one hundred. Furthermore, I kept closely related styles to take advantage of economies of scale when purchasing raw materials, manufacturing services, and shipping and handling. For instance, with my highly specialized jewelry collection, I could contact just a handful of suppliers specializing in gemstones to get the highest quality at the lowest prices delivered quickly. Can you imagine contacting one hundred different suppliers to source gemstones worldwide? I used to be up all day and night speaking to miners from Asia, Africa, and North and South America. I used to source a variety of pearls and opals from Australia, Tahiti, and the Philippines. Getting rid of the styles I couldn't be the absolute best in simplified my team's duties and my own life.

Additionally, by specializing in only a few types of gemstones, I could negotiate much better prices from my suppliers due to the larger quantities I could buy. A typical supplier's delivery time and prices can change dramatically depending on your buying quantity. For example, in the gemstones business, a jeweler who buys one stone at a time might pay as high as $50 per carat for a London blue topaz. However, the same London blue topaz stone could be bought as low as $4.50 per carat for quantities of a thousand pieces or more. So, a London blue topaz stone weighing five carats could cost a jewelry supplier anywhere between $22.50 to $250 per piece. When I reduced the number of styles, my business lost a few customers, but we could attract much larger customers with less effort and see better profit margins. Besides, being laser-focused on my strength allowed me to spend much more time with my employees and family.

To see this in the real world, evaluate different companies in your market sector. Look at those companies that started small and scaled to become internationally recognized brands. For example, can you imagine Kentucky Fried Chicken expanding their menu to include sushi, stir-fry, meatloaf, and more? I do not think so. KFC knows its industry and their customer, therefore, they focus on the menu items that only enhance their core product of chicken, such as coleslaw, biscuits, and gravy. Following this strategic plan, KFC has remained on top of countless other chicken franchises.

In small ventures, your core business is typically what got your business started and what you're passionate about. Take the time to reflect on your core purpose and focus your efforts on scaling your business effectively. It is essential to consider how adding new products or services will impact your core business before adding them. At all costs, avoid "shiny new product" syndrome. Adding new products that directly compete with existing products is a common mistake among inexperienced entrepreneurs. I've seen it too many times. When gold prices escalated from $380 to $1,600 per ounce, many independent jewelers started offering the same styles in silver, brass, stainless steel, and other materials to help reduce costs. As a result, they provided various versions of the same styles with different price points—$1,500 for 14K gold, $129 for silver, $45 for brass, and $19 for stainless steel. That's a great way to confuse a customer. Before scaling up, ensure you have a clear competitive advantage in your core business.

SYSTEMIZING
Scaling a business isn't just about expanding upward and outward, it's also about optimizing your resources, internal processes, and operations. A weak infrastructure can lead to losing customers you've worked hard to acquire. It is crucial to remember that some systems and processes that worked when your business was in its infancy won't work when you attempt to scale. You may need to tweak strategies as your business grows, so adaptability and flexibility are essential. Developing a framework of what works and keeps your business running smoothly is vital to scaling a business.

Make your business as efficient and error-free as possible by automating and systemizing as much as possible. Creating systems for various parts of your business is worth the investment if it results in predictable financial results. For example, consider McDonald's french fries. According to the company, McDonald's has a systematic, predictable, and consistent formula that results in great fries every single time. This is why you can go to any McDonald's and get the same quality fries you love.

When I started my business, I oversaw everything: accounting, sales, and customer service. When I trained new staff, I provided them with an elementary procedural booklet at each workstation so they could look up certain tasks and learn how to perform them correctly. However, this was far from a simple system of aggressive growth. For example, on each purchase order, we had to manually calculate the fluctuating gold prices and indicate the color of the gold. It was cumbersome and not consistent.

In 1989, before the Internet age, my employees took orders by phone, and after they finished, they had to write down all the information before taking the next call. I began systemizing our ordering process after an employee made the simple mistake of writing white gold instead of yellow gold on a purchase order, a mistake that cost over $100,000. Changing our ordering system took several months, as our style numbers had to be converted to include the specific color of gold to alleviate the risk of ordering the wrong color gold. In addition, I developed a computer program that can automatically calculate the fluctuation in gold prices each day. While it is unnecessary to systemize every aspect of your business, you must systemize the core functions before scaling. Systemization improves efficiency and consistency and eliminates errors, reducing costs and mistakes.

INNOVATING
Small business owners often confuse the word *innovate* with the word *invent*. In my experience, the most meaningful innovation

happens when you improve products or services you already have. Webster's Dictionary defines innovation as a "new idea, method or device."[2] For example, do you remember when travel luggage, even some of the most expensive brands, wasn't offered with wheels? Over the years, I've traveled millions of miles, and I'll never forget seeing the first set of wheeled luggage. It was at a kiosk at JFK International in New York, and even though it was expensive, unattractive, and small, I purchased one before flying home. Soon, other luggage manufacturers added wheels as an innovation, which combined two existing products, luggage and wheels, and didn't require any scientific invention. So while some companies create products and services that didn't exist before, most businesses use innovation to improve their existing products in relevant ways.

Continue adapting and innovating to maintain your competitive advantage. To grow, you must consistently add innovation to your core products. Innovation may involve the manufacturing process or finding ways to make your products easier or more efficient for your customers.

I have found ways to innovate even in the jewelry business, one of the world's oldest industries. For example, when I started my jewelry business in 1989, necklaces were available in standard lengths of eight, twenty-four, and thirty inches. However, I learned through my customers that many women preferred sixteen- or seventeen-inch necklaces. Most customers didn't want to buy multiple lengths of chains. There were many manufacturers I contacted. I had to plead with them to make a sixteen-inch necklace with a three-inch extender built in so that the customer could wear it at any length up to nineteen inches, clasping it at the desired length. The campaign was a huge success, and my company Ravello Beverly Hills gained a reputation for innovation.

When planning upgrades to your existing projects in the spirit of innovation, be creative but be grounded as well. Be sure the innovations you are planning are cost-effective and sustainable. By choosing mindful, sustainable solutions for your business, you can ensure its long-term viability.

CONTINUOUS INNOVATION

The consumer experience of your core products must be enhanced by adding significant improvements as you go. Referring to the luggage and wheels example, they were initially unsightly and small, and the wheels did not operate smoothly. Since this emergent innovation, many luggage manufacturers have elevated their products, improved their offerings, and led the charge in scaling their business. Manufacturers now offer TSA-approved luggage with tamper-proof locks that are lightweight, made with durable materials, and have exceptionally organized compartments. In addition, wheeled luggage with USB-type chargers is now available from many premium luggage brands. Innovation is never enough if you only do it occasionally. To remain competitive, you must continually improve all aspects of your core products through consistent innovation and adaptability to the marketplace.

DOMINATE YOUR INDUSTRY

By identifying your core products, developing your clear competitive advantage, and consistently adding innovative features, your products become the go-to choices among your target audience. Once this happens, your company will thrive as you dominate the specific industry or product category.

Regardless of your business's size or industry dominance, you must never become complacent. Once market domination takes shape, the hard work truly begins. Whenever your innovations reach market success, expect many competitors to copy your ideas and claim that their products are superior to yours. The key is to be vigilant and consistently stay ahead of your competition.

CHAPTER 15

KEY TAKEAWAYS

- Regardless of your business's size or industry dominance, you must never become complacent.

- To scale, you need to strengthen your core business, the part where you have a competitive advantage.

- Continue adapting and innovating to maintain your competitive advantage.

- The customer experience of your core products must be enhanced by adding significant, sustainable improvements as you grow.

CHAPTER 16

Embark on Your Journey—Your Pathway to Millions

Just when the caterpillar thought the world was over, it became a butterfly.

—ENGLISH PROVERB

MY HOME IN CALIFORNIA IS SPACIOUS AND COMFORTING, almost nest-like, and I sit here reminiscing about my life, this book, and this closing chapter. The house is a peaceful and quiet haven, filled with the influences of my parents, who taught me to chase my dreams and never give up on my passions, despite the hardships and mistakes that may come along the way. This book was inspired by the extreme difficulties and fears I faced throughout my life and how I triumphed over them. I can only imagine the thoughts, feelings, and even heartache my parents felt leaving their comfortable life in South Korea for a new life in the United States. My father bravely and boldly followed his passion, wanting nothing more than an opportunity to provide a better life for his family. Even after arriving in the United States and discovering that every penny of our assets was frozen, my father never wavered and never gave up.

Even though he didn't show it, I imagine now that he must have felt genuine fear, confusion, and doubt. But he was excited to embark on a new journey in the United States. As we settled into our new lives, facing difficult challenges, we persevered. I developed the emotional fortitude needed to change my life. Every day, I witnessed my father fight fires that threatened to engulf him, but no blaze burned brighter than the fire inside of him. Nothing could extinguish it. There were many days when it seemed his world was crashing, but he never gave up hope for his family. Instead, he struggled and came out better on the other side.

The thirty-five years I have spent in retail have been filled with obstacles and mistakes. Despite giving my business my absolute best, I have to admit that, more than once, my best wasn't enough. Even though I have contemplated closing my business, I could not give up on my dreams. To survive, I've had to pivot and evolve multiple times. But, most importantly, I dared to dream and, against all odds, found a way to realize that dream. In my unique journey, my improbable success fueled my desire to help others pursue their passions. If a penniless immigrant can achieve the American Dream simply by pursuing her passion, anyone can do it.

The life you dream of can be lived with hard work, determination, and the willingness to learn from your mistakes. Neither money nor fame defined success in my family. In my mind, success has everything to do with happiness and quality of life, not money. As I share what I have learned on my journey, I believe I can help others achieve their version of success. Despite this internal drive, I didn't have a detailed plan to write the book until recently. My schedule was hectic, and I never had time to sit down and put pen to paper. Besides, I wasn't sure the strategies I'd developed and implemented over the years would benefit today's entrepreneurs. But business leaders, colleagues, friends, and family encouraged me to write a book to help struggling entrepreneurs.

What I loved most about being on HSN and other channels was connecting with millions of women every month, and it wasn't just jewelry sales that formed. We, the millions of viewers and I, built and nurtured bonds through our shared experiences: a strong affection for our children, passion for our careers, exciting milestones, and overcoming obstacles. The time I spent with HSN was a true gift, and I wouldn't trade those years for anything, but it was time to move on. So, in 2017, I left HSN, stepping into a new phase of my life.

After writing my first science fiction novel, I presented it to literary agents and major publishers who provided expert, constructive criticism and encouragement. As a result of my live TV shows, several editors and publishers recognized me. Many of them were avid fans of my jewelry and encouraged me to write this how-to book. I had the opportunity to write a book about building a successful career and business based on my story. Yet, initially, I resisted because I felt it was just another story about resilience and survival. Originally, I was unsure if I had anything earth-shattering to share, but then it occurred to me that most of us are dreamers and work hard to achieve our goals. I thought of the people who would roll up their sleeves and work diligently to achieve their dream of owning their own business but wouldn't know where to begin. And the more I considered the book, the more I realized that the systems and processes I learned throughout my years could help them.

As I got to work writing, I knew I had to dive deep and offer an in-depth look at what it takes to start and maintain a business. As a new entrepreneur, I hope you use this book to guide your passion into a dream business. I want this book to be a beacon of hope for you, your friends, family, and colleagues who want to start their businesses. Life-changing endeavors can be scary, thrilling, and overwhelming, but also rewarding. Starting a business without money or expertise is difficult. Still, it is possible, and as I have shown in these pages, success is more about mindset and attitude than money or status. The path to success results from hard work and determination, being innovative, creative, wise, and agile in the marketplace. You already possess everything you need to succeed.

I want to share some final points and hopeful takeaways you should carry for the rest of your business days. We crave authentic human interaction as our lives become increasingly dependent on technology. And in today's world, people increasingly do business with people with whom they identify, like, and respect. There is no substitute for an honest, humble, and compassionate person doing their best to serve their customers, no matter how much knowledge, marketing, or advertising they have or use. Ultimately, consumers want to do business with companies that care about their employees, customers, communities, and the environment. With family and business, there's no choice, and family comes first. When faced with a choice between family and passion, remember that your mission is to always be present for your family.

The everyday race and momentum of your business can be overwhelming when you're starting. In 1998, nearly every segment of my business was booming, and I realized I spent much more time away from my family growing my business than I had ever expected. Traveling several hundred thousand air miles was hectic and exhausting, so I actively sought ways to simplify my life without sacrificing income. Having my TV show on HSN (on a trial basis) posed financial risks, but I took it in order to spend more time with my family. I'd only need to travel once a month to HSN's studio, and I could hire other people to handle some of my other clients. And even though I expected some of my business segments to drop, an unexpected chain of events occurred, and my business grew. Each time I purposely tried to escape from certain portions of my business, somehow, I made more money and had more time. You can too.

Remember your humble beginnings when your business consumes everything in your life, and prioritize your family over money, business, and fame. You will enjoy higher-quality personal time and exponential profit growth.

Be a contrarian, work hard, and believe in yourself. Never underestimate your creativity and ingenuity, but learn from those who have gone before you. Never accept the first results as final. Instead, take on all challenges and keep going. Would the Wright brothers have invented airplanes had they accepted the status quo? Can you imagine your world without the greatest inventions made possible by astounding never-quit inventors such as Albert Einstein, Alexander Graham Bell, Thomas Jefferson, and even Ben Franklin, all of whom never accepted what was in front of them and brought us electricity, medicine, microwaves, music, and digital technology, which were made possible by refusing to let the status quo stand?

Without dreamers and innovators like Steve Jobs or Bill Gates, would you even own a mobile phone or sit in front of a computer and see people around the world? And without visionaries like Amazon's Jeff Bezos, who continues to think creatively, would you even be reading this book you ordered yesterday? Instead, they reached deeper within, often through thousands of failures, only to emerge the victor on the other side. So reach deeper within yourself, never settle, or assume the first mistake or failure is the end game and definitive answer. Instead, push further, look harder, and when you need to break the rules, don't be afraid to do so.

Finally, I would like to touch on one aspect I feel is vitally important. Some individuals often refer to the concept of divine purpose as karma. When I was a little kid, my parents told me that karma comes back, good or bad, with interest. So choose wisely, be respectful, and help others whenever possible because your honorable deeds will multiply good fortune if you strive to be the best person you can be to others and yourself.

Creating something you are passionate about is a journey of self-discovery and growth. It can be a central way to not only make a living but also make a positive impact on the world. And along the journey, you will learn invaluable lessons about yourself, your industry, and your world. But expect unfortunate detours, distractions, peaks, valleys, and unsolicited bad advice from naysayers. So get past it and rise above by never giving up on your mission, despite what happens.

You can turn your passion into a successful million-dollar business by working hard, persevering, and being dedicated. Remember that family comes first; divine intervention and karma will take care of your business. Your new business will provide a rewarding journey that lets you pursue your passions and create something of which you will be proud. Your work will transcend time, reaching many long after you are gone. Let nothing stand in your way of making a difference and changing the world. Follow your passion with vigor, and like the caterpillar turned butterfly, take wing and soar. I wish you Godspeed on your business journey toward the pinnacle of million-dollar success.

Thank you for letting me share my journey with you.

—Victoria Wieck

ACKNOWLEDGMENTS

"Happiness" and "success" are terms that many people use inter-changeably, and they often believe that achieving success will bring them happiness. Happiness and success are indeed connected, but they are not interchangeable. History is filled with highly successful individuals in virtually every profession—artists, entertainers, politicians, scientists, the list goes on—who lived without attaining happiness. I discovered in my journey that the key to everything in life is learning to be happy. When I was climbing the corporate ladder after graduating with a master's degree in business, everyone, including myself, believed I was highly successful. I had a dream job with a good salary, an excellent benefits package, and a lot of upward mobility, but I was miserable. One day, I told myself that I was never going to get rich. I needed to find a way to spend my time doing what I was naturally good at—something I could enjoy doing and also earn enough money to sustain my lifestyle. Only after I made a decision to live the life I wanted to live, instead of the life I thought I had to live to make ends meet, my life changed forever. I was able to spend ample time with my family and still achieve professional success beyond my wildest dreams.

In the early years of my journey, I had to find ways to motivate myself to keep working toward a better future when profits were very slim. Most important to me was my strong relationship with my family, which was the primary source of my motivation, inspiration, and resilience. This book is my endeavor to motivate millions of moms, dads, inventors, and creatives to believe in themselves and create their future.

To my husband, Kevin, my soulmate, best friend, and partner in every facet of my life, thank you for your unshakable love. This book wouldn't have been possible without your help and belief in me. Through all the hard times, you were always there by my side, lifting me up. I wouldn't be who I am today without you. Nothing that matters in my life would have been possible without you.

To my children, Rachel and KJ, you are the source of my greatest joys and my reason for living. I always strove to be a good mother above anything else. I treasure your love and support, and I thank you for encouraging me to write this book.

To my parents, thank you for sacrificing everything and immigrating to the United States to secure a better life for your children. You taught me some of the most essential things in life—love, honesty, persistence, and courage to do the right thing, not the easy thing.

To my business colleagues worldwide, especially those at HSN, where I spent nineteen years as a TV personality, I thank you for your support, friendship, and guidance. Our time together, every minute, was a true gift that I will cherish for the rest of my life. I was blessed to have spent those years with all of you.

To the millions of customers of the Victoria Wieck Jewelry brand, my journey wouldn't be complete without your support, and this book wouldn't have been possible without you. Your loyalty, feedback, and love for my designs mean the world to me.

For the production of this book, I thank my literary agent, Gary Krebs, for his belief in me and his help in helping me share my story. I thank him for his guidance and for never giving up. I thank my editor, Jeffrey Mangus, for all his efforts—wordsmithing, editing, and adding finishing touches to the book. I also thank everyone at Rowman & Littlefield for bringing my dream book to light so that I can help others transform their lives for the better.

Notes

Introduction
1. James Truslow Adams, *Epic of America* (Boston: Little, Brown, and Company, 1931).

Chapter 1
1. Noel Tichy and Ram Charan, "Speed, Simplicity, Self-Confidence: An Interview with Jack Welch," *Harvard Business Review*, September/October 1989. Accessed April 2023. https://hbr.org/1989/09/speed-simplicity-self-confidence -an-interview-with-jack-welch.
2. About Google: Commitments, Google, accessed May 20, 2023, https:// about.google/commitments.
3. About Instagram: Instagram, accessed May 20, 2023, https://about .instagram.com.
4. About LinkedIn: Culture and Values, accessed May 20, 2023, https:// careers.linkedin.com/culture-and-values.
5. Edwin A. Locke, "Toward a Theory of Task Motivation and Incentives," *Organizational Behaviour and Human Performance* 3, no. 2 (1968): 157–89. https: //doi.org/10.1016/0030-5073(68)90004-4.
6. Paul B. Brown, "'You Miss 100% of the Shots You Don't Take.' You Need To Start Shooting At Your Goals," Forbes, January 12, 2014. https://www.forbes .com/sites/actiontrumpseverything/2014/01/12/you-miss-100-of-the-shots -you-dont-take-so-start-shooting-at-your-goal/?sh=21d4c79c6a40.

Chapter 2
1. Dan Schawbel, "Seth Godin Urges You to Poke the Box," Forbes, March 1, 2011. https://www.forbes.com/sites/danschawbel/2011/03/01/seth-godin-poke -the-box-interview/?sh=563c24b976ad.
2. "22 Fear of Failure Statistics to Change the Way You Think," Soocial, n.d.. https://www.soocial.com/fear-of-failure-statistics.

3. Mandy Hale, *The Single Woman: Life, Love, and Dash of Sass* (Nashville, TN: Thomas Nelson, 2013).

CHAPTER 3

1. Steve Jobs, commencement address at Stanford University, June 12, 2005.
2. Stephen King, *On Writing: A Memoir of the Craft* (New York: Scribner, 2010).
3. S. Hubner, M. Baum, and M. Frese, "Contagion of Entrepreneurial Passion: Effects on Employee Outcomes," *Entrepreneurship Theory and Practice* 44, no. 6(2020). https://doi.org/10.1177/1042258719883995.
4. Elizabeth Gilbert, *Big Magic: Creative Living Beyond Fear* (London: Penguin Publishing, 2015).
5. "Warren Buffet Joins Levo League to Elevate Careers of Gen Y," BusinessWire, May 7, 2013. https://www.businesswire.com/news/home/20130507007338/en/Warren-Buffett-Joins-Levo-League-to-Elevate-Careers-of-Gen-Y.
6. Steve Jobs, commencement address at Stanford University, June 12, 2005.

CHAPTER 4

1. Vincent Lombardi, statement made as coach of the Green Bay Packers, 1959.
2. "Nationwide Ad Featuring 'Dead' Child Is Most Controversial of Super Bowl," Fox Sports, February 2, 2014. https://www.foxsports.com/stories/nfl/nationwide-ad-featuring-dead-child-is-most-controversial-of-super-bowl.

CHAPTER 5

1. Matthew Kirby, *Icefall* (New York: Scholastic, 2013).
2. Nicolas Cole, "7 Reasons Why People Give Up on Their Goals Too Early," *Inc.*, March 3, 2017, https://www.inc.com/nicolas-cole/7-reasons-people-give-up-on-their-goals-too-early.html.
3. *Merriam-Webster*, s.v. "courage (n.)," accessed August 29, 2023. https://www.merriam-webster.com/dictionary/courage.
4. Steve Jobs, commencement address at Stanford University, June 12, 2005.

CHAPTER 6

1. Howard Shultz, *Pour Your Heart into It: How Starbucks Built a Company One Cup at a Time* (New York: Hachette Books, 1999).
2. "'Brad's Drink' Becomes Pepsi-Cola, 1898," North Carolina Department of Natural and Cultural Resources, August 28, 2016. https://www.ncdcr.gov/blog/2016/08/28/brads-drink-becomes-pepsi-cola-1898.
3. Tom Huddleston Jr., "5 of Jeff Bezos' Best Lessons for Success from His 27 Years as Amazon CEO," CNBC Make It, July 5, 2021. https://www.cnbc.com

/2021/07/05/jeff-bezos-best-lessons-for-success-from-his-27-years-as-amazon
-ceo.html.

4. "Vrity, the New Brand Measurement Company for the Values Economy,
Announces Launch of the Values Return Index (VRI)," GlobeNewsWire,
March 1, 2021. Accessed August 29, 2023. https://www.globenewswire.com/
news-release/2021/03/01/2184379/0/en/Vrity-the-New-Brand-Measurement-
Company-for-the-Values-Economy-Announces-Launch-of-the-Values-Re-
turn-Index-VRI.html.

5. Idowu Koyenikan, *Wealth for All: Living a Life of Success at the Edge of Your
Ability* (Fuquay-Varina: Grandeur Touch, LLC, 2016).

CHAPTER 7

1. Robert Lewis Stevenson, *Virginibus Puerisque and Other Papers* (London: C.
Kegan Paul & Co., 1881).

2. Felix Richter, "The Generation Gap in TV Consumption." Statista, November 20, 2020. https://www.statista.com/chart/15224/daily-tv-consumption-by
-us-adults.

3. Pooka Agnihotri, *17 Reasons Why Businesses Fail: Unscrew Yourself from
Business Failures* (self-pub, 2021).

CHAPTER 8

1. Simon Sinek, *Start with Why: How Great Leaders Inspire Everyone to Take
Action* (Edmonton: Portfolio, 2009).

2. *Merriam-Webster's Collegiate Dictionary*, s.v. "marketing (*n.*)." Accessed June
17, 2023. https://unabridged.merriam-webster.com/collegiate/marketing.

3. Sherman Standberry, "The Importance of a Website for Your Business
Success," Lyfe Marketing, June 15, 2022. https://www.lyfemarketing.com/blog/
importance-of-a-website.

4. Sandvine, "Sandvine's 2023 Global Internet Phenomena Report Shows
24% Jump in Video Traffic, with Netflix Volume Overtaking YouTube," Cis-
ion: PR Newswire, January 17, 2023. Accessed August 29, 2023. https://www.
prnewswire.com/news-releases/sandvines-2023-global-internet-phenomena-
report-shows-24-jump-in-video-traffic-with-netflix-volume-overtaking-you-
tube-301723445.html.

CHAPTER 9

1. Warren Buffet, letter to Berkshire Hathaway Investors, 2008. https://
tradebrains.in/warren-buffet-price-is-what-you-pay-value-is-what-you-get.

2. Sumit Aggarwal, "The Moment You Make a Mis-
take in Pricing, You're Eating into Your Reputation or Your Profits," LinkedIn, April 13, 2018. https://www.linkedin.com/pulse/
moment-you-make-mistake-pricing-youre-eating-your-profits-aggarwal.

3. Michael Marn V. and Robert L. Rosiello, "Managing Price, Gaining Profit," *Harvard Business Review*, September/October 1992. https://hbr.org/1992/09/managing-price-gaining-profit.

4. Chan W. Kim and Renée Mauborgne, *Blue Ocean Strategy: How to Create Uncontested Market Space and Make the Competition Irrelevant* (Boston: Harvard Business Review Press, 2015).

CHAPTER 10

1. John F. Kennedy, inaugural address, January 20, 1961.

2. PON Staff. "10 Top Negotiation Examples," Program on Negotiation, Harvard Law School, September 26, 2019. https://www.pon.harvard.edu/daily/negotiation-skills-daily/famous-negotiators-feature-in-top-negotiations-of-2012.

3. "How Much of Communication Is Nonverbal?" The University of Texas Permian Basin, 2023. https://online.utpb.edu/about-us/articles/communication/how-much-of-communication-is-nonverbal/#:~:text=It%20was%20Albert%20Mehrabian%2C%20a,%2C%20and%207%25%20words%20only.

CHAPTER 11

1. Sun Tzu, *The Art of War* (Boston & London: Shambhala, 1988).

2. Neil Patel, "90% Of Startups Fail: Here's What You Need To Know About The 10%," Forbes, January 16, 2015. https://www.forbes.com/sites/neilpatel/2015/01/16/90-of-startups-will-fail-heres-what-you-need-to-know-about-the-10/?sh=307f6aa86679.

3. Marcus Cook, "The Biggest Misconceptions on Why Startups Fail," *Inc.*, April 27, 2021. https://www.inc.com/marcus-cook/the-biggest-misconception-on-why-startups-fail.html.

4. Masroor Agnedm, "Is Social Media the Biggest Influencer of Buying Decisions?" *Social Media Today*, May 28, 2015. https://www.socialmediatoday.com/marketing/masroor/2015-05-28/social-media-biggest-influencer-buying-decisions.

CHAPTER 12

1. Celinne Da Costa, "3 Reasons Why Brand Storytelling Is The Future of Marketing," Forbes, January 31, 2019, https://www.forbes.com/sites/celinnedacosta/2019/01/31/3-reasons-why-brand-storytelling-is-the-future-of-marketing/?sh=4a44e62555ff.

2. "Half of American TV Viewers Watch 10 or More Hours of TV during the Week," Ipsos, July 28, 2021. https://www.ipsos.com/en-us/news-polls/american-tv-viewing-habits-2021.

3. Kendall Haven, *Story Proof: The Science Behind the Startling Power of Story* (Santa Barbara, CA: Libraries Unlimited, 2007).

4. Douglas Van Praet, *Unconscious Branding: How Neuroscience Can Empower (and Inspire) Marketing* (New York: St. Martins Griffin, 2014).

5. Michael Fertick, "As Trust Among Consumers Wavers, Authenticity is Critical," Forbes, January 14, 2019. https://www.forbes.com/sites/michaelfertik/2019/01/14/as-trust-among-consumers-wavers-authenticity-is-critical/?sh=4d01867872a4.

6. Marketwired, "A Minute of Video Is Worth 1.8 Million Words, According to Forrester Research," Yahoo! Finance, April 17, 2014. Accessed August 29, 2023. https://finance.yahoo.com/news/minute-video-worth-1-8-130000033.html.

CHAPTER 13
1. Daniel Lovering, "Oprah Winfrey Tells Harvard Graduates to Learn from Mistakes," Reuters, May 30, 2013. https://www.reuters.com/article/entertainment-us-usa-harvard-oprah/oprah-winfrey-tells-harvard-graduates-to-learn-from-mistakes-idUSBRE94U01020130531.

CHAPTER 15
1. "Jack Welch on Pursuing Your Passion," Edcor, https://www.edcor.com/newsletter/jack-welch-on-pursuing-your-passion.

2. *Merriam-Webster's Collegiate Dictionary*, s.v. "innovation (*n.*)." Accessed June 18, 2023. https://unabridged.merriam-webster.com/collegiate/innovation.

INDEX